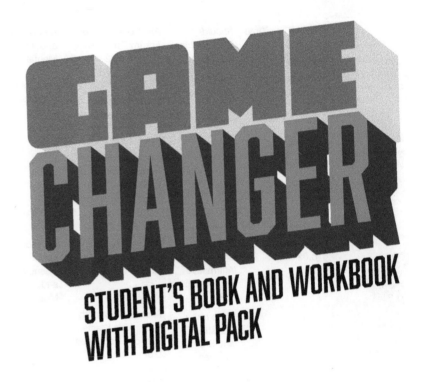

GAME CHANGER

STUDENT'S BOOK AND WORKBOOK
WITH DIGITAL PACK

3

VIVIANE KIRMELIENE, DENISE SANTOS,
LIZ WALTER AND KATE WOODFORD WITH PAULO MACHADO

CAMBRIDGE
UNIVERSITY PRESS

CONTENTS

* This material can be downloaded from the Digital Resource Pack.

WELCOME!

COMPARATIVES

1 Complete the article with the comparative form of the adjectives in parentheses.

Visit Rio de Janeiro

Carnival celebrations in Brazil are ¹ _more exciting than_ (exciting) in any other country, and Rio de Janeiro is Brazil's most popular destination with a lot of different neighborhoods to choose from. For example Ipanema is famous for its Carnival parties, but it's ² _____ (crowded) Barra da Tijuca, and Santa Tereza is ³ _____ (traditional) both those neighborhoods – you'll definitely enjoy an authentic "carioca" experience there!

In Rio you'll want to have fun at the beach, too! Copacabana and Leblon are amazing, but beaches like Prainha, Reserva, and Grumari are often ⁴ _____ (clean) and ⁵ _____ (peaceful) those very popular beaches.

After enjoying the Carnival, you can visit places not too far away from Rio. Petrópolis, Itaipava, and Penedo are a lot ⁶ _____ (quiet) the state capital, and are great places to relax!

GERUNDS

2 Complete the mini dialogues with the gerund form of the verbs below.

- add   - avoid   - ~~drink~~   - ride   - take   - wait

1 **A** Dr. Ramirez, what are some things people can do to keep healthy?

   B Well, _____drinking_____ enough water is very important. And _____ sugar is a simple step. For example, _____ more sugar to chocolate milk is totally unnecessary.

2 **A** I don't like _____ the bus to school.

   B Why? It's much faster than _____ your bike.

   A Yes, but I don't like _____ for the bus on my own at the bus stop.

FREE-TIME ACTIVITIES

3 🔊 0.01 Look at the images and complete with the words below. Then listen, check, and repeat.

- eat   - go   - ~~play~~   - watch

_____play_____ in a band   _____ out   _____ to a concert   _____ series

4

OCCUPATIONS

1 🔊 **0.02 Put the letters below in the correct order and label the images. Then listen, check, and repeat.**

- ~~ahsinof snedegir~~ • camisuni • hefc • lheteta • nraced • regeenni • suern • taorc

1 fashion designer

2

3

4

5

6

7

8

SIMPLE FUTURE

2 **Complete the sentences with the correct simple future form of the verbs in parentheses.**

1 The inventor _____will explain_____ (explain) his new project in the next class.

2 We can have a picnic at the park on Sunday. I'm sure it _____ (not rain).

3 The students _____ (donate) their old books to the local library.

4 My cell phone still works well, so I _____ (not buy) a new one for the moment.

5 _____ Julia _____ (live) abroad like her sister?

BE GOING TO

3 **Write questions using the prompts and the correct form of *be going to*.**

1 How long / you / stay at school today?

_____

2 you / do your homework immediately after class?

_____

3 What time / you / get up tomorrow?

_____

4 What / you / do next vacation?

_____

🗣️ USE IT!

4 **Work in pairs. Take turns asking and answering the questions in Exercise 3.**

> How long are you going to stay at school today?

> I'm going to be here until 2 p.m. What about you?

EXTREME WEATHER

1 🔊 **0.03 Complete the sentences with a word from each box. Then listen and check.**

• ~~blizzard~~ • heatwave	• flood • hurricane	• forest fire • thunderstorm		• ~~cold~~ • incredible	• dry • terrible	• hot • wet

1 It was really _____cold_____ here yesterday and a _____blizzard_____ hit the city in the morning.

2 We arrived in Madrid during a _____. It was really _____ in the afternoon.

3 A _____ can start quickly in a summer with no rain, when the country is very _____.

4 Because of the _____, everything downstairs in our house got _____.

5 There was a big _____ in Perth last night. Look at the _____ photo my cousin took!

6 The _____ caused _____ problems for people living on the coast.

PRESENT PROGRESSIVE

2 Complete the dialogue with the correct present progressive form of the verbs in parentheses.

A My brother and his friend ¹_____are leaving_____ (leave) for Australia next month.

B Wow! How long ²_____ they _____ (stay) there?

A For six weeks. They ³_____ (come) back at the end of August.

B ⁴_____ your sister _____ (work) in the mall tonight?

A No, she isn't. She ⁵_____ (study) for a test.

POLITE OFFERS

3 Write questions to ask a friend using the prompts and the correct object pronoun.

1 There's a new science fiction movie at Moviemark. (see?)

_____

2 My dad made these chocolate cookies. (try?)

_____

3 We're playing video games at Isa's house tonight. (join?)

_____

 LOOK!

We use the present progressive for future plans, appointments, and arrangements.

Mariela **is traveling** to the UK next week. (She has her plane ticket and her hotel booking.)

4 Complete the sentences with *I'd like to* or *I'd love to* and your own ideas.

1 _____ go _____ tonight.

2 _____ meet _____ one day.

 USE IT!

5 Work in pairs. Take turns saying your sentences in Exercise 4 and asking questions to find out more information.

I'd like to go to the movies tonight.

What would you like to see?

SHOPPING

1 🔊 **0.04 Circle the correct options. Then listen and check.**

Olivia is at the ¹*shop /* (*shopping*) / *store* mall. She'd like to buy a new jacket, but she can't ²*donate / earn / afford* it. She ³*saved / spent / borrowed* almost all her ⁴*pocket / customer / free* money last weekend, and she can't use her ⁵*money / debit / bargain* card because she doesn't have enough ⁶*money / bills / coins* in the bank.

COUNTABLE AND UNCOUNTABLE NOUNS

2 **Complete the chart with the words below.**

- artist
- beauty
- border
- food
- information
- juice
- message
- money
- price
- review

Countable	Uncountable
artist	

INTENSIFIERS

3 **Circle the correct options.**

1 I put (*too much*) / *too many* sugar in my coffee.
2 Lucas is the most popular student I know. He has *a lot of / enough* friends.
3 The test was difficult. There were *too much / too many* questions to answer.
4 This closet is so small! There's *enough / not enough* space for your clothes.
5 There's *not much / not many* information about Carl's accident. I hope he's OK.
6 You don't need to go to the market. We have *enough / too many* eggs for the cake.

QUANTIFIERS

4 **Complete the sentences with *How much* or *How many*.**

1 ___How much___ homework did you do last night?
2 _____ water do you drink every day?
3 _____ students are there in your science class?
4 _____ time do you need to get to school?
5 _____ people live in your home?
6 _____ subjects do you study?

 LOOK!

In affirmative sentences, we use *a lot of*, not *much*.

There's **a lot of** food in the fridge.

I have **a lot of** homework to do.

 USE IT!

5 **Work in pairs. Take turns asking and answering the questions in Exercise 4.**

FESTIVALS AND CELEBRATIONS

1 🔊 0.05 **Complete the sentences with the words below. Then listen and check.**

- atmosphere
- crowds
- dance shows
- fireworks
- music events
- ~~souvenirs~~

1. Many tourists like to buy _____souvenirs_____ at street markets.
2. Everyone danced and laughed a lot at Grandma's party. The _____ was great!
3. _____ of people enjoy the Carnival at Copacabana.
4. Women wear traditional dresses in _____ in India.
5. _____ are a popular way to celebrate the New Year all over the world.
6. According to the reviews, PopParty Fest was one of the best _____ of the year.

DEFINING AND NON-DEFINING RELATIVE CLAUSES

2 **Write one sentence with a non-defining relative clause using the two sentences and *who* or *which*.**

1. I watched the game with Bruna. Bruna is a big soccer fan.
   ----

2. The Paragon is closed this week. The Paragon is our favorite café.
   ----

3. Hiro lives in Portugal now. Hiro is Japanese.
   ----

4. Last month I joined the drama club. The drama club meets every Tuesday at 2 p.m.

ADVERBS OF MANNER

3 **Complete the sentences with adverbs from the adjectives in parentheses.**

1. Sophia walked _____carefully_____ (careful) around the gift store because she didn't want to break anything.
2. Isabela is a fantastic role model because she studies _____ (hard).
3. Mrs. Silva was driving too _____ (fast) in the snowy weather.
4. The teacher told us to think _____ (creative) to solve the math problem.
5. Santiago doesn't play volleyball very _____ (good) but he's a wonderful coach.

USE IT!

> I always ride my bike very carefully.

> I think that's true.

4 **Work in pairs. Think of two true sentences and one false sentence about you using the adverbs in Exercise 3. Take turns saying your sentences and guess which of your partner's sentences is false.**

1
MY LIFE PLAN

UNIT GOALS

- Talk about life stages and studying.
- Read a blog about studying English abroad.
- Listen to a video class giving tips for studying.
- Learn about saving indigenous languages.
- Express certainty and uncertainty.

THINK!

1 What do you think is happening in the image?

2 Is learning English important for situations like the one in the image? Why / Why not?

VIDEO

1 Say three things in the video that are amazing.

2 Which invention helped us to connect the whole world?

VOCABULARY IN CONTEXT

LIFE STAGES

1 🔊 **1.01 Read the quiz and match the words and phrases in bold with images 1–10. Then listen, check, and repeat.**

What is the most important thing in your life plan?

DO THE QUIZ TO FIND OUT.

A Will you **go to college** when you **finish school**?

⭐ ☐ No way. I'll **get a job** and earn my own money.

⭐ ☐ Yes, of course. I want to keep studying to learn more about the world.

⭐ ☐ I'm not sure. Maybe I'll **take a course** to get more practical skills.

B Which option best describes you?

⭐ ☐ To be happy I need to be able to help in my community.

⭐ ☐ I'll never **retire** – I want to work for the rest of my life.

⭐ ☐ When I'm an adult, I want to **get married** and **have children**.

C For you, what's the most important thing about learning English?

⭐ ☐ It helps me make new friends.

⭐ ☐ When I **take an exam** in English, I want to get a good score.

⭐ ☐ It connects me with other people around the world.

D What worries you the most when you think about the future?

⭐ ☐ Not finding a job after I **graduate**.

⭐ ☐ Being alone when I **leave home**.

⭐ ☐ Pollution and climate change.

1
finish school

2

3

4

5

6

7

8

9

10

2 Do the quiz and check (✓) your answers. Then look at your score below and discuss it with a partner. Do you agree with your results? Why? / Why not?

Most of your answers are ...	The most important thing in your life plan is ...	
⭐	WORK	You're hard-working and always busy! You'll be successful, but never forget that the people around you are very important, too.
⭐	PEOPLE	You're a sociable person and you love to be around people. That's great, but remember: there's a big world out there, too!
⭐	THE WORLD	You think big and have great plans, but try to also find time for your private life. It's important to have some fun!

3 Complete the chart with the words and phrases below.

- finish school
- ~~get a job~~
- get married
- go to college
- graduate
- have children
- leave home
- retire
- take a course
- take an exam

Work	Education	Family
get a job		

4 Complete the sentences so they are true for you. Use words and phrases from Exercise 3.

1 I'm going to _____ before I leave home.
2 I think I'll be busy when I _____.
3 I'm going to _____ after I _____.
4 I don't think I'll _____.
5 I'm not going to _____ before I'm 35.
6 When I _____, I'll be really happy.

> **LOOK!**
>
> After *when*, *before*, and *after* to talk about the future, use the simple present, not *will*.
> When I **get** a job, I'll save some money.

 USE IT!

5 Work in pairs. Take turns asking and answering about your future. Replace the phrases in bold with the correct form of other words and phrases from Exercise 3.

> Do you think **going to college** is important?

> What do you want to do after you **finish school**?

> Do you want to **get married**?

> Yes, I do.

> I want to take a course.

> I'm not sure.

READING

WORKBOOK p.115

LEARN&LIVE ENGLISH

HOME | OUR COURSES | DESTINATIONS | STUDENT LIFE | **BLOG** | CONTACT US

LET'S WELCOME OUR NEW STUDENTS VERÓNICA GONZÁLEZ AND DANIEL RIBEIRO!

Verónica, 14
From: Mexico
♥ video games and sports

WHY MALTA?

Some years ago I saw a video about the Maltese coast and I loved it! When I learned that English is one of the two official languages in Malta, I thought, "I want to study English there."

Most people speak English and **Maltese** here. I can't speak Maltese, but I can read the street signs – because **they** use English, too!

EXPECTATIONS

I think I'll have a great time here in Malta. I'm going to take a four-week English course. Later, who knows? Will this experience help me get a job in the future? Maybe. I'd love to become a game developer, so maybe I'll make games about Malta!

ABOUT US

We offer a variety of English courses for teenagers (12–17) in different countries.

Daniel, 15
From: Brazil
♥ languages and big animals

WHY SOUTH AFRICA?

My parents wanted me to study English abroad before I go to college, and my dream is to go on a safari, so we decided that South Africa seemed like the perfect place.

I found out that there are **over** ten official languages in South Africa. English is one of **them** and most people **actually** speak English as a second language here.

EXPECTATIONS

I'm very excited about this course. We're not going to sit in a classroom all day. Tomorrow our instructors are going to take us to a local village. We're going to help build a school there. How cool is that?

1 Read the text quickly and circle the sentences that are true.

1 The text is a magazine article about English courses in different countries.

2 There are three blog posts on the page.

3 The people in the images are going to start an English course.

4 This website is for teenagers who want to study English abroad.

2 🔊 1.02 Read and listen to the text. Then answer the questions. Write *V* (Verónica), *D* (Daniel), or *B* (both).

Who …

1 likes wild animals? ___D___

2 is in a country where English is one of the official languages? _____

3 is going to take a course that lasts for a month? _____

4 is going to do some community work as part of the course? _____

5 chose the country after talking to family members? _____

6 hopes that the experience abroad will be useful in the future? _____

3 Look at the words in bold in the blog post and circle the correct options in sentences 1–5.

Verónica
1 "Maltese" refers to a (language spoken in)/ *person from* Malta.
2 The word "they" refers to *people from* / *street signs in* Malta.
3 The word "over" means *more than* / *on top of*.

Daniel
4 The word "them" refers to *official languages in* / *people from* South Africa.
5 It is possible to replace "actually" with *at the moment* / *in fact*.

THINK!

How many of these countries have English as an official language: Australia, Bahamas, Guyana, Ireland, Pakistan, Singapore, Uganda? Why do you think English is an official language in so many countries?

 WORKBOOK p.115

LANGUAGE IN CONTEXT

1 Look at the examples below. Complete the sentences from the blog post.

	Will for Predictions	*Be going to* for Intentions
Affirmative **(+)**	I think I ¹_____ a great time here in Malta. I'm sure this course **will teach** Verónica a lot.	Our instructors ³_____ us to a village. He**'s going to** help build a house.
Negative **(–)**	The classes **won't be** boring. She probably **won't want** to leave Malta!	We ⁴_____ in a classroom all day. Bill **is not going to** spend the summer here.
Questions **(?)**	²_____ this experience _____ me get a job?	When **are** you **going to leave** South Africa?

2 Put the words in the correct order.

1 probably / I'll / a / children / lot / have / of
   ~~I'll probably have a lot of children.~~

2 think / next / graduate / I / will / my / year / cousin
   _____

3 to / are / retire / my / going / soon / grandparents
   _____

4 you'll / better / maybe / tomorrow / feel
   _____

5 next Monday / we're / have / going / not / to / classes
   _____

 LOOK!

We often use *will* with *I believe, I (don't) think, I'm sure, maybe, perhaps, probably.*

Maybe one day I**'ll** visit Malta.

3 Look at Daniel's diary for next week. Complete the sentences with the correct form of *be going to.*

	MONDAY	TUESDAY	WEDNESDAY	THURSDAY	FRIDAY	SATURDAY & SUNDAY
WEEKLY PLANNER	classes until 12:30 go bike riding	classes until 12:30 11:15 go bird watching	Sports Day	classes until 12:30 go swimming	classes until 12:30 go on a safari	go on a safari visit Cape Town

1 Daniel ~~is going to play sports~~ on Wednesday. (+)
2 The students _____ on Thursday afternoon. (+)
3 Daniel _____ after 11:15 on Tuesday. (–)
4 In a message to his parents, Daniel wrote, "I _____ on Tuesday afternoon." (+)
5 _____ Daniel and his friends _____ on Saturday? No, they're not.
6 _____ Daniel _____ four days next week? Yes, he is.

 USE IT!

4 Complete the sentences with the correct forms of *be going to* so they are true for you.

1 When I leave home, _____ . (+)
2 One thing about my life in the future: I _____ . (–)

5 Work in pairs. Take turns reading your sentences and making comments.

> That's great! You'll have a lot of fun!

LISTENING AND VOCABULARY

1 Look at the images. Check (✓) what you think the topic of the video class is.

1 ◯ How to do your homework quickly.

2 ◯ How to learn and make friends at the same time.

3 ◯ How to be successful when you take a course.

4 ◯ How to learn English online.

2 🔊 1.03 Listen to the teacher's introduction to the video class and check your answer to Exercise 1.

3 🔊 1.04 Listen to the video class and complete the captions with the words/phrases below.

• get a good grade   • ~~make progress~~   • practice   • prepare   • review   • take a break

1 Teacher

Tips to help you __make progress__ in this course.

2 Fernando

_____ every thirty minutes or so.

3 Melody

Use the Internet to _____ your skills.

4 Raquel

Use cards to _____ vocabulary.

5 Alejandro

I give myself a lot of time to _____ for an exam.

6 Cataline

Do you want to _____ _____ in this course?

4 🔊 1.05 Listen, check, and repeat your answers to Exercise 3.

5 🔊 1.04 Listen to the video class again and write *T* (true) or *F* (false).

1 The teacher gives five suggestions. __F__

2 The suggestions are only useful for learning English. _____

3 One of the students thinks it's easier to learn when you often stop to rest. _____

4 Three students mention technological devices in their suggestions. _____

5 One of the students talks about another person's idea. _____

6 Match the students in screens 2–6 with these sentences.

1 Recording yourself on your phone can help you a lot. _____

2 Leaving everything to the last minute is a bad idea. _____

3 When you don't stop for short periods, you get too tired. _____

4 You can write your own bilingual dictionary. _____

5 Listening to podcasts and writing comments about what you hear is a good idea. _____

✏️ **WORKBOOK** p.113

LANGUAGE IN CONTEXT

1 Complete the sentences from the video class in the chart. Use the words below.

• herself   • myself   • yourself   • yourselves

Reflexive Pronouns	
Singular	**Plural**
I give ¹_____ a lot of time to prepare for an exam. **You** need to give ²_____ some time to rest. **She** recorded ³_____ reading the new words. **He** enjoyed **himself** in his English class. **The computer** will turn **itself** off soon.	**All of you**, get ⁴_____ ready for some great tips. **We** gave **ourselves** some time to rest. **The students** saw **themselves** on the screen.

2 Complete the sentences with the correct reflexive pronoun from the chart. Then underline the expression that means *alone*.

1 My friend and I enjoyed _____ourselves_____ at the concert.
2 The teacher asked the students, "How much time did you give _____ to prepare for the exam?"
3 Eve is very independent, she wants to do things by _____.
4 Use this knife but be careful, Ben cut _____ with it last week.
5 My car can park _____ – it's really helpful when I go downtown.
6 I'm teaching _____ to play the guitar. It's more difficult than I thought.

> **LOOK!**
> *By + myself, yourself*, etc. means *alone, on one's own*.
> I usually do my homework **by myself**.

3 Circle the correct options.

1 **Ren** I think George will be an artist when (he)/ *himself* grows up.
  Lottie Yes, I agree. He knows how to express *him / himself* in his drawings.
2 **Mom** You're 14, Ben! It's important to know how to take care of *you / yourself*.
  Ben Yeah, but I do. I look at *me / myself* in the mirror every day to make sure *I / myself* look fabulous.
  Mom Very funny, Ben, but I'm talking about your health. You need to take *it / itself* seriously.
3 **Frank** What's the matter with Maria? She's talking to *her / herself*.
  Karla There's nothing wrong with that. People often talk to *them / themselves*.

4 Write sentences in your notebook using words and phrases from charts A, B, and C.

A	B	C	
I	enjoy	myself	herself
My best friend and I	laugh at	yourself	ourselves
My friends from school	listen to	himself	themselves
My dad/mom/sister (etc.)	talk to		

_____My dad often talks to himself when he's cooking._____

 USE IT!

5 Work in pairs. Ask questions using *yourself* and verbs from chart B in Exercise 4.

Do you test yourself before an exam? | Yes, I do.
Did you enjoy yourself at the party? | Yes, I did.

 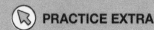

Home | **Posts** | About me

Maori Teenager Becomes Language Influencer

By *Lawrence O'Brien*

KIA ORA!

"Maori is part of our cultural identity," says Turei Rarere.

1 **HASTINGS, NEW ZEALAND** – You look at Turei Rarere and you see a cheerful teenager like many others. When you talk to him, you understand why he is an influencer. Turei is smart, creative, and motivated.

2 "Two years ago, there was a party in my family, and I realized my younger cousins didn't speak Maori," He explains. "And worse – they didn't think that was a problem! I was really surprised. Didn't they understand that Maori is part of our cultural identity?" This question motivated Turei to create an online group for indigenous teenagers to discuss how they felt about their native languages.

3 Three years later, Turei's group has hundreds of members. It is not only a group for discussion, but also a place to learn and practice indigenous languages from around the world. "We use English to talk to a large number of people, but we use our native languages to post videos or audio with traditional stories or songs."

Ko Taraika ahau

A Maori graffiti

4 Alexandra Silva, a 15-year old Brazilian from the Terena people, says she feels more connected to her community now. "I grew up speaking Portuguese. Turei's group helped me understand why Terena is important. I can understand my grandparents' stories now."

5 Turei is certain about his plans for the future. "My aunt is a Maori teacher in our local school. I'm going to follow in her footsteps. I'm planning to go to college to study linguistics and I'll always support people who want to teach or learn indigenous languages."

1 Read the article quickly and check (✓) the correct answers.

1 The topic of the article is …
   a ◯ the Maori language.
   b ◯ keeping languages alive.
   c ◯ the importance of the Internet.

2 The article's main idea is that teenagers…
   a ◯ can help make their culture stronger.
   b ◯ learn languages more quickly than adults.
   c ◯ are spending too much time online now.

2 ◁)) 1.06 Read and listen to the article. Check your answers in Exercise 1.

3 Read the article again. Match a–e with paragraphs 1–5 in the article.

a an introduction about Turei ____1____

b a description of Turei's online activity _____

c an example of how Turei's idea is helping people from other countries _____

d the event that gave Turei an idea _____

e what Turei wants to do when he leaves school _____

WORDS IN CONTEXT

4 Replace the words/phrases in bold with words/phrases in the article. Use a dictionary to check your answers.

1 What are the **original, native** languages in your country? ____indigenous____

2 Turei likes to **help** people who want to learn their grandparents' language. _____

3 My mother started her own business and I'm going to **do the same thing**. _____

4 When I talked to Turei, I **understood for the first time** he was a special teenager. _____

5 Turei is **sure** about what he wants to do in the future. _____

5 Match 1–6 with a–f.

1 Alexandra _____
2 English _____
3 Maori _____
4 Terena _____
5 Turei _____
6 Turei's aunt _____

a is an indigenous language teacher.
b is an official language in New Zealand, together with English.
c is an indigenous language in Brazil.
d is useful for connecting people all around the world.
e can use the native language of her community now.
f wants to teach Maori in the future.

THINK!

Why do you think the teenagers sometimes interact in English in Turei's group?
Do you think it's important to know English to exchange ideas with people around the world?

WEBQUEST

Check (✓) the numbers you think are correct.

There are around _____ indigenous languages in Papua New Guinea. The country recognises _____ languages as official languages.

◯ 850/4   ◯ 1000/8   ◯ 550/2

VIDEO
1.2

1 Which three languages do Tomasz and Veronique's children speak?

2 How many languages are there in Nigeria?

SPEAKING

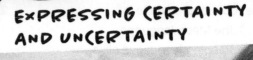 EXPRESSING CERTAINTY AND UNCERTAINTY

1 🔊 **1.07 Read and listen to Vanessa and Martina. What course are the girls discussing?**

Vanessa	This is so cool! I think I'll study robotics when I leave school.
Martina	Oh really? Is that how you see yourself ten years from now? Making robots?
Vanessa	Definitely! I know I'm good at this, and I love it. What about you?
Martina	Well, I'm not sure. I don't really know much about robotics, but yeah, maybe I'll go for it, too.

LIVING ENGLISH

2 **Match the expressions (1–3) with their meanings (a–c).**

1 definitely _____   a I think it's possible
2 I'm not sure _____   b I'm certain
3 maybe _____   c I'm uncertain

3 🔊 **1.08 Listen and repeat the expressions.**

PRONUNCIATION

4 🔊 **1.09 Listen and pay attention to the pronunciation of 'll and will.**

I'll study robotics in college.
People **will** use robots at home.

5 🔊 **1.09 Listen again and repeat.**

6 🔊 **1.10 Do you hear 'll or will? Listen to six sentences and write 1–6 in the chart.**

'll	will
1	

7 🔊 **1.07 Listen to the dialogue again. Then practice with a partner.**

8 **Role play a new dialogue. Follow the steps.**

1 Change the words in blue to write a new dialogue in your notebook.
2 Practice your dialogue with a partner.
3 Present your dialogue to the class.

 YOUR DIGITAL PORTFOLIO

Record your dialogue and upload it to your class digital portfolio.

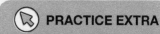 PRACTICE EXTRA

2

WHAT MAKES US HAPPY?

UNIT GOALS

- Talk about free-time activities, and health and fitness.
- Read posts on an online advice forum.
- Listen to a podcast about the mental benefits of exercising.
- Learn about the positive effects of art.
- Write a forum post giving advice.

THINK!

1 Why do you think the teenagers are happy?

2 What are two things that make you happy?

VIDEO

1 What three countries have very happy people?

2 What makes people in Norway happy?

VOCABULARY IN CONTEXT

MORE FREE-TIME ACTIVITIES

1 🔊 **2.01 Complete the pamphlet about vacation activities for teenagers with the words and phrases below. Then listen, check, and repeat the phrases for activities.**

- board games
- ~~cookies~~
- gymnastics
- jewelry
- models
- singing lessons
- skateboarding
- sunset
- walk
- yoga

VACATION TIME! / What can teenagers do in OAKLAKE VIEW?

Our city offers a lot of great activities for teenagers during school vacations. Check out some activities at our community center and at Green Park.

OAKLAKE VIEW COMMUNITY CENTER

[1] **Bake** _____cookies_____ in our kitchen. Yummy!

[2] **Make** _____ in the workshop.

[3] **Take** _____ with our music teacher.

Try a new sport – [4] **do** _____ with our winning team!

Have fun with your friends! Come and [5] **play** _____ or [6] **build** _____.

GREEN PARK

[7] **Go** _____ at the best skate park in town.

Relax and enjoy nature. You can [8] **do** _____ or just [9] **take a** _____.

[10] **Watch the** _____ at the end of the day.

2 Label the images with the correct activities from Exercise 1.

......play a board game......

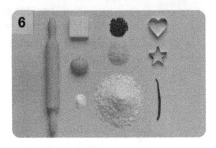

----

3 Read the mini dialogues. What activities from Exercise 1 are the teenagers doing?

1 Coach Hands together, Jack! Keep your arms and legs straight!

   Jack Yes, coach!

----

2 Teacher Right, Melissa. Let's try again. The final note is higher.

   Melissa OK. La-la-la …

----

3 Fernanda Look at all those colors in the sky!

   Lucas Yeah, it's beautiful!

----

4 Laura Which way do you want to go?

   Martin Let's go down past the lake. I want to see the water birds.

----

4 Complete the chart with the phrases for activities 1–10 in Exercise 1.

Activities I Often Do	Activities I Would Like To Do	Activities I'm Not Interested In

 USE IT!

5 Work in pairs. Take turns asking and answering questions about your information and your partner's information.

> Do you often take a walk?

> No, I don't, but I'd like to.

READING

The Teen Oracle The place for no-nonsense advice from teens to teens

Home | Lifestyle | School work

Sleepy Teen
Level: Apprentice II
Questions: 6
Replies: 12

I'm sooooo tired – I feel sleepy every day, all the time. I have a lot of responsibilities – besides school from Mon to Fri, I bake cookies to raise money for our class trip at the end of the school year and I help at an animal shelter on Sat and Sun. I hardly ever see my friends and never have time to go skateboarding, the only physical activity I really enjoy. I love studying, baking, and helping animals, and I don't want to disappoint others. What should I do? ¹............

↪ REPLY

↪ **Delphi**
Level: Teen Oracle III
Questions: 24
Replies: 112

IMO, you're doing too much. If you're feeling tired and your health is OK, it's clear you should reduce the number of activities in your routine. How about asking for help? Your classmates should bake all of the cookies for a change. And maybe you should go to the animal shelter only on Saturday or Sunday. ²............

 👍 LIKE

↪ **MelindaT**
Level: Teen Oracle I
Questions: 18
Replies: 76

When I feel I have too much on my plate, making a list of activities helps me decide on priorities. Maybe a relative or your BFF can help you with that. One important thing: you shouldn't stop exercising, even if you just take a quick walk. Should you go skateboarding? Yes, you should! ³............

 👍 LIKE

1 Look at the online forum. Check (✓) its purpose.

1 ◯ to give advice to teenagers who have problems
2 ◯ to give suggestions for free-time activities for teenagers

2 🔊 **2.02** Read the forum posts and complete them with the missing sentences (a–c). Then read, listen, and check.

a Being active will definitely make you feel better.
b That way you'll have some time for yourself.
c The thing is, I simply don't have time to relax anymore.

3 Read the forum posts again. Check (✓) the names in the chart.

Who ...	Sleepy Teen	Delphi	MelindaT
1 wants to sleep all the time?	✓		
2 believes physical activity is important?			
3 gives advice about asking for help?			
4 is afraid of making people sad?			
5 thinks writing a list is a good idea?			
6 gives advice about reducing responsibilities?			

THINK!

Delphi and MelindaT gave advice to Sleepy Teen.
Which piece of advice do you think is better? Why?

✏ **WORKBOOK** p.119

LANGUAGE IN CONTEXT

1 Look at the examples below. Complete the sentences from the forum posts.

Should/Shouldn't for Advice		
Affirmative (+)	**Negative (–)**	**Questions (?) and Short Answers**
You ¹ _____should_____ reduce the number of activities in your routine. Sleepy Teen **should** go skateboarding. Your classmates ² _____ bake all of the cookies.	You ³ _____ stop exercising! She **shouldn't** go to the shelter on Sunday. Her parents **shouldn't** allow her to have so many activities.	⁴ _____ you go skateboarding? Yes, you ⁵ _____. / No, you **shouldn't**. **Should** she stop baking cookies? Yes, she **should**. / No, she **shouldn't**. What ⁶ _____ I do? Who **should** she ask for help?

2 Complete the sentences with *should* or *shouldn't*.

1 If you have trouble concentrating at school, you _____should_____ try to do yoga every morning.
2 Your dog behaves badly because he's bored. You _____ take him to the park every day.
3 Dante's grades are low. He _____ spend more time on his school work.
4 People _____ drive fast on the roads when it's foggy.
5 Isabella is checking her cell phone for messages. She _____ do that in class.

> 🔍 **LOOK!**
>
> **Don't use *to* with the verb after *should*.**
>
> I think you **should do** yoga every morning.

3 Look at the images. Write sentences with *should* and *shouldn't* using the words below.

- eat so much junk food
- listen to loud music on the train
- go to bed early
- ~~study late at night~~
- have some fruit
- turn the volume down

1 _Ava shouldn't study late at night. She should_ _____
2 _____
3 _____

 USE IT!

4 Work in pairs. Imagine you have one of the problems below. Ask your partner for advice.

- You feel anxious before school tests.
- You feel tired all the time.
- You're late for school every morning.
- You're having problems with homework.

> I feel anxious before school tests. What should I do?

> I think you should …

LISTENING AND VOCABULARY

1 Read this podcast. Match the <u>underlined</u> expressions with the definitions (1–6).

HEALTHY TEENS PODCAST

Episode #33

May 7

13 min

Mental Health Benefits of Exercising for Teens

0:00:00

For this episode, we asked the question "**Why do you <u>work out</u>?**" Here are some answers from followers:

"Yoga helps me <u>reduce stress</u>. I have a busy life, but I sleep better on the days I do yoga." – Sophia, 14

"When we do physical activities, our brain produces chemicals that make us happy. I feel great every time I <u>go for a run</u>." – Syed, 15

"I play soccer to <u>stay fit</u> and have fun! And playing any team sport is a great way to <u>make friends</u> – you meet people that like the same things as you." – Mika, 13

"I know working out is good to <u>prevent diseases</u>. I have asthma, and swimming is very good for my health." – Jiro, 14

0:13:00

1 do an activity where you move fast ...._go for a run_...........
2 keep your body strong and healthy ....
3 do physical exercise ....
4 feel less anxious ....
5 stop medical problems from happening ....
6 start friendships with other people ....

2 🔊 2.03 Listen, check, and repeat your answers to Exercise 1.

3 Check (✓) the places you think the podcast host visited to talk to teenagers.

○ a mall   ○ a park   ○ a school gym   ○ a café

4 🔊 2.04 Listen to the podcast and check your answers to Exercise 3.

5 🔊 2.04 Listen again. Which of the actions 1–6 in Exercise 1 is <u>not</u> mentioned in the podcast?

6 Read the sentences and write *T* (true) or *F* (false).

1 Emma talks to two teenagers who are doing team sports. ....F....
2 The girl says running helps her do well on exams. ....
3 Emma and the girl agree that running reduces stress. ....
4 Emma talks to the PE teacher during a game. ....
5 The boy had more friends after he joined the basketball team. ....

✏️ **WORKBOOK** p.117

LANGUAGE IN CONTEXT

1 Complete the sentences from the podcast in the chart. Use the phrases below.

- can we?   • didn't it?   • don't you?   • isn't it?

Tag Questions			
Affirmative (+) Sentence	**Negative (–) Tag**	**Negative (–) Sentence**	**Affirmative (+) Tag**
It's a nice way to reduce stress,	1 _____	**Emma isn't** very fit,	**is she?**
Emma was talking with a runner,	**wasn't she?**	**We weren't playing** volleyball,	**were we?**
You also **feel** good after exercising,	2 _____	**The two teenagers don't know** Emma,	**do they?**
Basketball helped you make friends,	3 _____	**The girl didn't stop** to talk to Emma,	**did she?**
People can download the podcast,	**can't they?**	**We can't** escape PE,	4 _____

2 Match 1–6 with a–f.

1 You like to exercise, ___b___
2 Mike and Samuel aren't fit, _____
3 The students didn't have PE yesterday, _____
4 Hassan is going to take a walk in the park, _____
5 Exercising helps people feel better, _____
6 You can ride a skateboard, _____

a can't you?
b don't you?
c did they?
d are they?
e doesn't it?
f isn't he?

> **LOOK!**
> The negative tag for *I am* (*I'm*) is *aren't I?*.
> **I'm** a good friend, **aren't I?**

3 Kelly and Nori are talking about the podcast. Complete with the correct tag questions.

Kelly Emma Madison is the host of the podcast, 1 _isn't she?_

Nori Yes, she is. And she does a great job.

Kelly Yeah, I like her, too. She talked to two teenagers in the last podcast, 2 _____

Nori No, to six. When I called you yesterday, you were listening to the episode, 3 _____

Kelly Yes, I was, but I only heard the first five minutes. I need to write a report about it for my science class. According to Emma, people feel good after exercising, 4 _____

Nori Yes, but I'm not here to answer your questions, 5 _____ Why don't you download the episode?

Kelly I don't have time! You don't have classes right now, 6 _____

Nori No, but soccer practice starts in five minutes and I really need to go. Bye!

 USE IT!

4 Work in pairs. Complete the chart with guesses about your partner.

Two Things You Think He/She Did Last Week	Two Facts About His/Her Life	Two Things You Think He/She's Going To Do

6 Take turns asking your partner tag questions to find out if your guesses were correct.

> You went to the movies yesterday, didn't you?

> No, I didn't. My sister went to the movies. I stayed home.

✏ **WORKBOOK** p.116 **and** 118   🔍 **PRACTICE EXTRA**   **25**

CAN MAKING ART MAKE YOU HAPPY?

Art classes are usually fun, aren't they? Well, experts tell us that there are good reasons for that.

By David Hurley
March 12

- Making art increases activity at the front of the brain, which makes us feel positive. And just looking at works of art can release the "feel-good" chemical called dopamine in the brain.

- Making art is a way to express emotions. When you create any piece of art, you have an opportunity to understand your feelings and deal with emotions.

- Working with art also helps you to focus on the moment. Some people mention that when they are creating art, they don't feel tired or hungry — they lose sense of time.

We talked to two teenagers about how art helped them in difficult times.

"Last year I moved away from my hometown. The art teacher in my new school noticed how sad I was and invited me to her art workshops with other students after school. Creating art definitely helped me feel better. I especially love to model clay and make sculptures. Every time I work on a piece, I feel relaxed and peaceful."

Chloe, 15

"When I was going through a hard time last year, my mom bought a coloring book and pencils for me. At first, I found the idea ridiculous — she didn't think I was a little kid again, did she? But she persuaded me to give it a try. When I started coloring, I found that I could 'turn off' the outside world and only focus on filling the forms with color. And my problems didn't seem that bad when I got to the end. Coloring calms my mind when I'm anxious."

Lucas, 14

1 **Look at the article. Check (✓) its main topic.**

1 ◯ Tips for people who want to make art as a hobby

2 ◯ Mental health benefits of making art

3 ◯ How teen artists started to create works of art

2 **2.05** **Read and listen to the article. Which two works of art do you think Chloe and Lucas created? Write *C* (Chloe) and *L* (Lucas).**

3 **Read the article again. Complete the statements with the words below. There are three extra words.**

- anxious
- ~~brain~~
- emotions
- difficult
- mother
- pencils
- problems
- sculptures
- teacher
- understand

1 Creating and looking at art have a positive effect on the _____brain._____

2 Art can help people _____ their feelings.

3 Chloe's art _____ helped her when she was having a _____ time.

4 Chloe's favorite activity at the art workshops is making _____.

5 Lucas didn't like it when his _____ bought him a coloring book.

6 He feels better about his _____ when he finishes coloring.

WORDS IN CONTEXT

4 **Match the expressions from the article with their definitions.**

1 focus on _____

2 move away _____

3 go through _____

4 give something a try _____

a go to live in a new place

b attempt to do something new

c give a lot of attention to one particular person, subject, or thing

d experience something, especially something difficult

 THINK!

Choose one of the artworks on page 26 and this page. Think of four adjectives to describe it.

 WEBQUEST

Learn more! Check (✓) *True* or *False*.
Johanna Basford, the author of *Secret Garden*, and other coloring books, sold over 21 million copies of her books in the 2010s.

◯ True   ◯ False

 VIDEO

2.2

1 Say three emotions in the video.

2 What is the name of the chemical that makes us feel good?

 **WRITING**

1 Look at the posts. Who is asking The Teen Oracle for advice?

The Teen Oracle
The place for no-nonsense advice from teens to teens

Home | Lifestyle | School work

 Worried_Sis
Level: Apprentice I
Questions: 1
Replies: 1

Hi, everyone! I'm here because I need help. My brother Jake feels sleepy all the time. He doesn't play any sports and eats junk food. I want to help him, but I work long hours and I don't see him much. What should I do?

REPLY

↳ Delphi
Level: Teen Oracle III
Questions: 24
Replies: 112

Well, I don't think you should worry too much if Jake often wants to sleep. We need a lot of sleep when we're teenagers – it's part of growing up, I guess.

But I know that physical exercise helps me feel more energetic, even during boring classes at school. 😊 Maybe you should invite him to take walks with you – that way he can be more active and you two can spend time together.
My older brother works long hours too and, believe me, I miss him!

Jake's eating habits are bad. He should include fruit and vegetables in his diet. Why don't you cook some healthy meals or snacks together? Eating well will help him have more energy and you will have another moment to talk and be together.

👍 LIKE

2 🔊 **2.06** Read and listen to the posts and answer the questions.

1 What three things is Worried_Sis anxious about?

----

2 What three pieces of advice does Delphi give to Worried_Sis?

----

3 Does Delphi give reasons and examples to support his advice?

----

3 Write a post with different advice from Delphi for Worried_Sis.

1 Think of a piece of advice for each problem.
2 Support your advice with reasons and examples.
3 Find or draw an image for your avatar and choose a username.
4 Write the first version of your post. Use the words/phrases in the Look! box and the vocabulary from Unit 2.

4 Switch your forum post with a classmate and check his/her work. Use the checklist below.

○ avatar and username
○ advice for the three problems
○ reasons and examples for the advice

○ *should/shouldn't*
○ *I (don't) think* and *maybe*

LOOK!

When we give advice, we often make our point less direct by using *I (don't) think* and *maybe* before using *should*.

I think you should suggest a different type of exercise.

Maybe he should join a gym.

 YOUR DIGITAL PORTFOLIO

Edit your forum post and upload it to the class portfolio for everyone to see!

REVIEW
UNITS 1 AND 2

🗨 VOCABULARY

1 Complete the invitation with the correct simple past form of the verbs below.

- get married
- go to college
- ~~graduate~~
- have children
- retire

SAVE THE DATE!

We met on the day we ¹ _____graduated_____ from high school.

We ² _____ together and ³ _____ four years later.

We ⁴ _____ two amazing _____ and worked hard for over 40 years!

We ⁵ _____ last month and we would like to invite you to our retirement party on September 20. You are part of our history!

Luis & Sofia

2 Put the letters in the correct order to complete Patricio's New Year's resolutions.

- ¹ _____review_____ (iwerve) what I learned in school for 15 minutes every day.
- ² _____ (aperctci) the piano four times a week
- ³ _____ (akte a ekrba) from social media one day a week
- ⁴ _____ (tge a ogdo agedr) in math
- continue to ⁵ _____ (ekam) good _____ (rogsesrp) in English

3 Circle the correct options.

A What do you do to ¹(stay in shape)/ make friends?

B I have a healthy diet, and I ²prevent diseases / work out every day.

A It's a lovely morning. Would you like to ³reduce stress / go for a run along the beach?

B Yes, that's a great idea.

A We're moving to England next month. My mom's working on a program to ⁴prevent diseases / go for a run. I think it'll be hard to ⁵make friends / work out there.

B Don't worry. You're the most sociable person I know.

4 Write what the people are doing. Use the words/phrases below and the correct verbs in the present progressive.

- a board game
- ~~gymnastics~~
- skateboarding
- a walk
- yoga

1 Amelia _____is doing gymnastics._____

2 Beatriz _____

3 Rodrigo _____

4 Logan and Olivia _____

5 Wilson _____

5 Complete the sentences with the correct form of *will* or *be going to* and the verbs in parentheses.

1 My sister _____is going to get_____ (going to / get) a summer job this year.

2 _____ you _____ (will / leave) home when you finish school?

3 I'm learning Spanish and I _____ (going to / take) an important exam next month.

4 My brother loves languages. Perhaps he _____ (will / take) a course abroad in the future.

5 We _____ (not going to / get) married this year.

6 Match 1–6 with a–f.

1 Did Maria enjoy ____f____

2 Do you look at _____

3 My parents are teaching _____

4 I'm not sure I can express _____

5 Pablo likes to review for exams _____

6 My friends and I gave _____

a myself clearly in English.

b themselves to play tennis.

c ourselves three weeks to prepare for the party.

d yourself in the mirror before you go out?

e by himself.

f herself at the beach last Sunday?

7 Put the words in the correct order. Then match images A and B with two pieces of advice.

1 scientist / should / a / you / become

_____You should become a scientist._____

2 yourself / you / by / go / shouldn't / camping

_____

3 more / be / should / patient / try / you / to

_____

4 teacher / should / your / help / for / you / ask

_____

5 spend / shouldn't / all / you / money / your

_____

A

B

8 Complete the sentences with tag questions.

1 You love building models, _____don't you?_____

2 Your friends took singing lessons last year, _____

3 Brenda isn't on the basketball team, _____

4 Arthur can make jewelry, _____

5 Your mother didn't bake cookies for the party, _____

6 I'm your best friend, _____

CHECK YOUR PROGRESS

I CAN ...

• talk about life stages and studying

• use *will* for predictions and *be going to* for intentions, and reflexive pronouns

• talk about free-time activities, and health and fitness

• use *should/shouldn't* for advice, and tag questions for confirming information.

3

CONSUMER WORLD

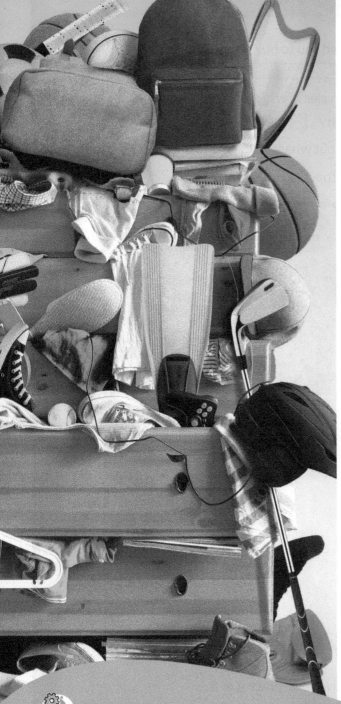

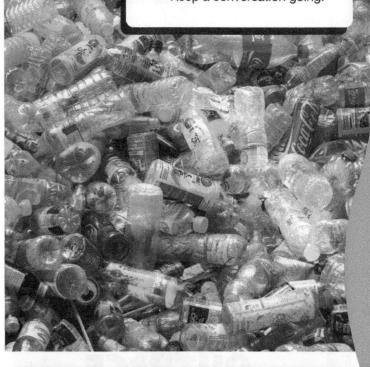

 UNIT GOALS

- Talk about advertising and money.
- Read about advertising techniques.
- Listen to a dialogue about spending money.
- Learn about a zero-waste project in Japan.
- Keep a conversation going.

THINK!

1 Is it a good idea to buy things at a secondhand store? Why / Why not?

2 What do you consider before you decide to buy something?

 **VIDEO**

3.1

1 Say two places where you can find adverts.

2 What helps you to remember a product in an advertisement?

VOCABULARY IN CONTEXT

ADVERTISING

1 🔊 3.01 Circle the correct words in the survey. Then listen, check, and repeat.

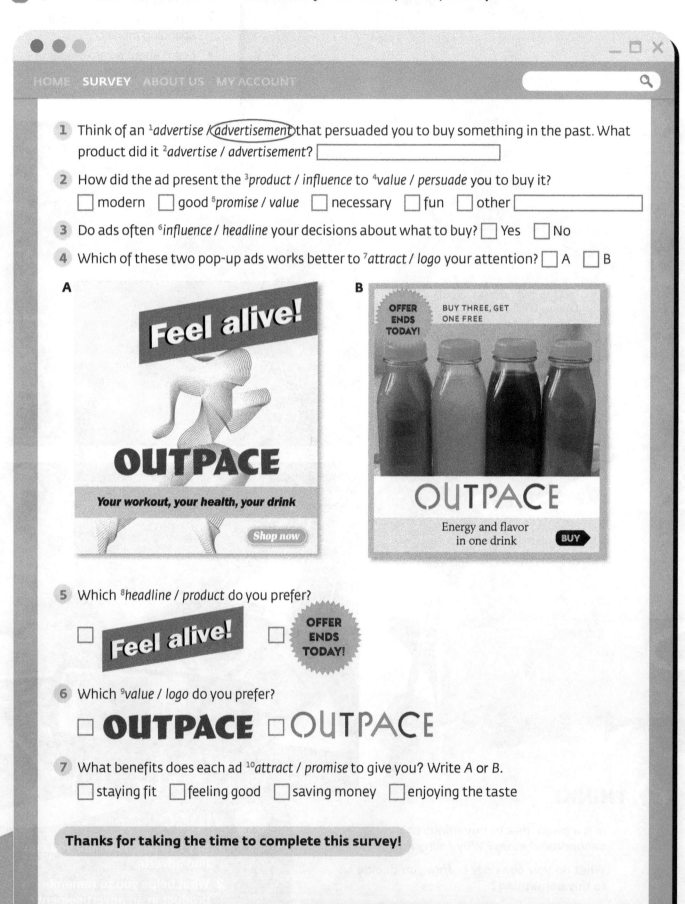

HOME **SURVEY** ABOUT US MY ACCOUNT

1 Think of an ¹*advertise /* ⟨*advertisement*⟩ that persuaded you to buy something in the past. What product did it ²*advertise / advertisement*? [   ]

2 How did the ad present the ³*product / influence* to ⁴*value / persuade* you to buy it?
☐ modern ☐ good ⁵*promise / value* ☐ necessary ☐ fun ☐ other [   ]

3 Do ads often ⁶*influence / headline* your decisions about what to buy? ☐ Yes ☐ No

4 Which of these two pop-up ads works better to ⁷*attract / logo* your attention? ☐ A ☐ B

A

Feel alive!
OUTPACE
Your workout, your health, your drink
Shop now

B

OFFER ENDS TODAY!
BUY THREE, GET ONE FREE
OUTPACE
Energy and flavor in one drink
BUY ▶

5 Which ⁸*headline / product* do you prefer?
☐ Feel alive!   ☐ OFFER ENDS TODAY!

6 Which ⁹*value / logo* do you prefer?
☐ **OUTPACE** ☐ OUTPACE

7 What benefits does each ad ¹⁰*attract / promise* to give you? Write A or B.
☐ staying fit ☐ feeling good ☐ saving money ☐ enjoying the taste

Thanks for taking the time to complete this survey!

2 Complete the survey in Exercise 1. Then share your answers with a partner.

3 Write *T* (true) or *F* (false).

1 The **product** in ads A and B is an energy drink. ____T____

2 The **logo** in ad A shows a person running. _____

3 Both advertisements are trying to **persuade** people to save money. _____

4 The **headline** appears at the bottom of a pop-up ad. _____

5 Ads often **promise** to improve our lives. _____

6 Every **advertisement** has an **influence** on people's decisions about what to buy. _____

7 Some ads **attract** us to the product by showing that it's not good **value**. _____

8 Companies **advertise** their products on the Internet, on TV, and on the radio. _____

4 Complete charts 1–3 with the words in bold in Exercise 1. Then match the charts with a or b below.

1 _____

Verb	Noun
persuade	persuasion
_____	attraction

2 _____

Verb	Noun
influence	_____
_____	promise

3 _____

Verb	Noun
advertise	_____

a The verb has the same form as the noun.　　b The verb and the noun forms are different.

5 Complete the sentences using the words in bold in Exercise 3. Then check (✓) the sentences that are true for you.

1 ○ I don't think ads _____influence_____ me but I like to watch them.

2 ○ I never believe ads that _____ to change my life.

3 ○ It's always easy to _____ my grandparents to buy what I want.

4 ○ I like to wear clothes that have a famous _____.

5 ○ Headlines in pop-up ads usually _____ my attention.

6 ○ Before buying a product, I often compare prices to make sure I get a good _____.

USE IT!

6 Work in pairs. Take turns asking and answering questions about the ideas in Exercise 5.

> Do you think ads ...?

> Do you believe ads that ...?

SMART TEEN

4 THINGS WE MUST NOT FORGET ABOUT ADS

by Mason Carlson

Do you sometimes decide to buy a product just because of an advertisement? Well, we all do. But here are some things to remember when we read or watch ads.

1 People produce ads to influence you

Behind all ads there are professionals who know what techniques will persuade us to buy. Even the funniest and most creative ads have one basic aim: to sell us something.

2 Ads want you to think you have to buy something – now!

Ads make you think you must act urgently: there's something fantastic out there and everyone else is enjoying it. And they also say it's easy to get it. Look! This burger is the "best" and "only" costs $3.99!

3 Ads use your emotions to get what they want

Are you worried about your friends thinking you're not attractive and cool? Ads show you beautiful, successful people having fun. Their idea? You buy what they advertise and you'll feel great, like the people in the ads.

4 Ads use famous people to attract you

Advertising companies pay a lot of money to celebrities. They know that fans will buy the product, not because they need it, but just because they love the star.

Comments

mei
I sometimes feel I have to buy something after I watch an ad. I buy it, I'm happy for a while, and then I want to buy something else.

👍 👎 reply

Blogger Boy

Ads don't influence me. You don't have to buy what they advertise.

👍 👎 reply

---

1 Look at the blog page and circle the correct options.

1 The blog Smart Teen is about *ads* / (*money*)

2 The people who write are *adults* / *teenagers*.

3 The readers are usually *adults* / *teenagers*.

4 Mason's post is about *advertising* / *allowances*.

5 Successful people *earn* / *save* a lot of money from advertising.

2 🔊 3.02 Read and listen to the blog post and comments. Check (✓) the correct answers.

1 What opinion does Mason have about ads?
  a ○ They influence us.
  b ○ They don't influence us.
  c ○ He's not sure about their influence.

2 Who disagree(s) with Mason in the comments?
  a ○ mei
  b ○ Blogger Boy
  c ○ mei and Blogger Boy

3 Read these people's comments during a meeting for an ad. Match them with 1–4 in the blog post.

a This will be a big hit with teens if we can persuade Taylor Swift to appear. ....

b We can start by asking, "Do you sometimes feel sad when you look at yourself in the mirror?" ....

c Let's go with the cartoon dog. If we can make people laugh, they'll feel good about the product. ....

d Let's end with "Hurry! This offer ends Saturday!" ....

 THINK!

Think of two ads you like. Do they use any of the techniques listed in the blog? If so, how? What other techniques do they use?

✏️ **WORKBOOK** p.123

LANGUAGE IN CONTEXT

1 Look at the examples below. Complete the sentences from the blog post.

Have to				Must		
Affirmative: Obligation				**Affirmative: Obligation**		
I/You/We/They	1 ----------------------------	buy something.		I/You/He/She/We/They	3 ----------------------------	act urgently.
He/She	**has to**					
Negative: No Obligation				**Negative: Prohibition**		
I/You/We/They	2 ----------------------------	buy what they advertise.		I/You/He/She/We/They	4 ----------------------------	forget four things about ads.
He/She	**doesn't have to**					

2 Match 1–5 with a–e. Then write the other form for obligation for the words in bold in a–e.

1 The students have an exam next week. __c__
2 Fernando is going to fly to Tokyo. _____
3 You started reading two hours ago. _____
4 Caroline wants to be a doctor. _____
5 This is a fantastic book. _____

a He **has to get** a passport. _____
b She **must study** hard. _____
c They **have to review** their lessons. ___must review___
d You **must take** a break. _____
e You **have to read** it. _____

3 Complete the sentences with *don't/doesn't have to* or *must not*.

1 You ___don't have to___ go now. You can stay here if you want.
2 She has a lot of clothes. She _____ buy a new skirt.
3 You _____ tell Ren about the party. It's going to be surprise.
4 The teacher said, "Put your phones in your bags. You _____ use them in class."
5 You _____ buy something just because it's a bargain.
6 He likes his job. He _____ look for a new one.

 LOOK!

We use *must not* to say something is the wrong thing to do.

You **must not forget** to do your homework.

 USE IT!

4 Complete the sentences so they are true for you.

1 When I'm in the library, I must not _____.
2 To get to school on time, I have to _____.
3 When I'm at home, I don't have to _____.
4 When I'm at school, I must _____.

5 Work in groups. Take turns reading your sentences in Exercise 4 to your group. Then tell the class one thing you have in common and one thing you don't have in common.

> When we're in the library, we must not talk on our cell phones.

> To get to school on time, Fernando has to get up at 6 a.m. The rest of the group don't have to get up so early.

LISTENING AND VOCABULARY

1 Look at the image. Check (✓) the words you think you will hear in the first part of the dialogue between Wilson and Diego.

1 ◯ afford
2 ◯ buy
3 ◯ expensive

4 ◯ money
5 ◯ price
6 ◯ spend

Diego

Wilson

2 ◁ 3.03 Listen to the first part of the dialogue and check your answers to Exercise 1.

3 ◁ 3.04 Diego and Wilson discuss how teenagers can make money. Look at these images. Whose ideas are they? Listen to the whole dialogue and write *D* (Diego), *W* (Wilson), or *N* (neither).

4 ◁ 3.04 Listen again and circle the correct options.

1 At the beginning of the dialogue, Wilson *wants* / *doesn't want* to buy new shoes.
2 Wilson *can* / *can't* afford the sneakers.
3 Wilson's parents think that we *must* / *don't have to* buy things because they are a good price.
4 Diego *agrees* / *doesn't agree* with Wilson's parents.
5 Diego gives Wilson some ideas about *donating* / *saving* money.
6 At the end of the dialogue, Wilson is *bored* / *excited* by Diego's suggestion.

5 ◁ 3.05 Match the words below with the definitions 1–6. Then listen, check, and repeat.

• cost • invest • label • on sale • own • ~~sell~~

1 opposite of *buy* _____*sell*_____
2 have, possess _____
3 company _____
4 with a reduced price _____
5 need payment of an amount of money _____
6 put your money into something that will produce more money _____

6 Complete the sentences with the words in Exercise 5.

1 Diego tells Wilson that the things we ____*own*____ don't have to be from a big _____.
2 Wilson's parents don't think it's always a good idea to buy things _____.
3 Diego thinks Wilson should save or _____ his money.
4 Wilson wants to make models and _____ them.
5 Cleaning materials don't _____ much.

36

✎ WORKBOOK p.121

LANGUAGE IN CONTEXT

1 Complete the sentences from the dialogue in the chart. Use the words and phrases below.

• does ... have to (x 2) • do ... have to • don't

Have to: Questions and Short Answers	
Do I have to use this product?	Yes, you **do**. / No, you **don't**.
1 _____ you _____ get them now?	Yes, I **do**. / No, I **don't**.
2 _____ everything _____ be from a big label?	Yes, it **does**. / No, it **doesn't**.
3 _____ we _____ buy everything that's on sale?	Yes, we **do**. / No, we ⁴_____.
How much **does** Diego **have to** spend on cleaning materials? When **do** they **have to** pay for the products?	

2 Complete the questions with the correct form of *have to*.

1 _____*Do*_____ you _____*have to*_____ go to bed early on Friday?
2 _____ we _____ add salt to the food?
3 _____ the owner of the store _____ invest money in big labels?
4 When _____ Ana _____ take her exams?
5 How many books _____ I _____ buy for this course?

3 Look at the chart. Then write questions using *have to* and short answers.

1 Juliana / exam?

----

2 Mateo / ATM?

Weekend To-do List	Juliana	Mateo
1 prepare for English exam	✓	✗
2 go to the ATM	✓	✗
3 finish school project	✗	✗
4 bake cookies	✓	✓

3 Juliana and Mateo / school project?

----

4 Juliana and Mateo / cookies?

USE IT!

4 Ask your classmates questions to find names for 1–5. Then ask *Wh–* questions (*what, where, why*, etc.) to get extra information and complete the chart.

Find Someone Who Has To ...	Name	Extra Information
1 get up early on Saturdays.		
2 help at home.		
3 buy something soon.		
4 save some money for something.		
5 take a bus home after school.		

> Do you have to get up early on Saturdays? Why do you have to do that?

> Yes, I do. Because I have soccer practice at 8 a.m.

HOME | ABOUT | PAST POSTS | WRITE FOR US

Rethinking Waste: Lessons From Japan

Some years ago, people in a Japanese village called Kamikatsu had the idea to go "zero waste." For this to happen, all residents would need to collaborate in important ways. A central idea in the project was the creation of a waste center where the residents had to take all their trash.

At first not everyone welcomed the idea because it involves a lot of work. Before going to the center, residents have to wash their non-organic trash, including plastic bags and bottles. At the center they have to put their waste in separate containers for different materials. There are 45 different categories of waste: for example, different places for different kinds of metal like aluminium and steel, and seven containers for paper, including newspapers, cardboard, and paper tubes. There are special places for toothbrushes, pillows, and furniture.

Nowadays, however, most people agree that the waste center is a great idea. Recycling makes money for the village. The fact that all waste is separated and cleaned adds value to it because it's easier to recycle. People also enjoy going to the *kuru-kuru* store in the center (*kuru-kuru* means "circular" in Japanese), where they can leave clothes, plates, or other useful items they don't want anymore. And a person who wants something from the store can take it away for free.

The village now recycles more than 80% of its waste but the project isn't only about recycling. As one of the organizers explained, "People have to avoid buying things that will go to waste. We must also avoid unnecessary packaging and try to use our own containers when possible." In other words, we must think about waste not only after we use something. We have to do it before use as well.

1 Look at the article: the title, image, and the first paragraph. Circle the correct options.

1 The words "waste" and "trash" *have / don't have* the same meaning.

2 A possible caption for the image is *Kamikatsu / Zero waste*.

3 The article is about a project to *spend less money / produce less waste* in a village.

2 🔊 **3.06** Read and listen to the article. Write *T* (true) or *F* (false). <u>Underline</u> the parts of the article that justify your answers.

1 There is a trash collection at all residents' homes in Kamikatsu. ___F___

2 At the beginning of the project not everyone liked the "zero waste" idea. _____

3 People have to put newspapers and cardboard tubes in the same place. _____

4 The village gets more money when it can sell clean waste. _____

5 It is possible to donate things at the center. _____

6 People can also buy recycled objects from the center. _____

WORDS IN CONTEXT

3 Match the words in bold in 1–4 with their definitions a–d.

1 Residents must separate **steel** from other types of metal. _____

2 They must avoid unnecessary **packaging**. _____

3 They mustn't put **cardboard** together with paper tubes. _____

4 They have to choose the correct **container** for all their waste. _____

a thick, hard paper, for example to make boxes

b materials used to cover products you buy

c object used for holding something

d very strong metal

4 Which image illustrates "We must also avoid unnecessary packaging and try to use our own containers when possible"?

5 Check (✓) the sentence that summarizes the main idea of the last paragraph.

1 ○ When you have new ideas, it's important to advertise them.

2 ○ When a city wants to do something, all residents must agree.

3 ○ It's possible to invent creative ways to use old materials again.

4 ○ Consumers must think about waste before they decide to buy something.

 ## WEBQUEST

Learn more! Check (✓) the correct answer.

Some stores use the letters BYOC to show they don't have any packaging for some products. What do these letters mean?

○ Borrow your own container

○ Bring your own container

○ Buy your own container

 ## THINK!

Think about something you bought recently. Did it have a lot of packaging? Did it create a lot of waste? Next time you buy something similar, what can you do to avoid unnecessary waste?

 ## VIDEO
3.2

1 When did people start to use plastic?

2 How much plastic waste gets recycled?

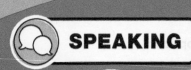

SPEAKING

KEEPING A CONVERSATION GOING

1 🔊 **3.07 Read and listen to Helen and Emilio. Where are they planning to go? Why?**

Helen Hey Emilio. It's Cristian's birthday tomorrow. We have to buy him a present.

Emilio Ah, OK, so let's go to the mall!

Helen Well, you know, I was thinking we could go to the secondhand store downtown.

Emilio What?

Helen Yeah, why not? We don't have to get an expensive present. I bet we'll find something special there.

Emilio Yeah, OK, I guess ... Maybe sports clothes or stuff like that ...

Helen Great. Let's go.

LIVING ENGLISH

2 **Match the expressions (1–3) with their meanings (a–c).**

1 Ah, OK, so	a I agree
2 Well, you know	b Yes, maybe, but I'm not sure
3 Yeah, OK, I guess	c I don't agree

3 🔊 **3.08 Listen and repeat the expressions.**

6 🔊 **3.10 Listen and circle the sound you hear: /f/ or /v/.**

1 I always **have** time for my friends. /f/ (/v/)
2 The students **have to** review for the exam. /f/ /v/
3 Liz doesn't **have** a lot of furniture. /f/ /v/
4 We **have** a lot of cousins – what about you? /f/ /v/
5 This is awful! We **have to** do something about it. /f/ /v/

7 🔊 **3.07 Listen to the dialogue again. Then practice with a partner.**

8 **Role play a new dialogue. Follow the steps.**

1 Change the words in blue to write a new dialogue in your notebook.
2 Practice your dialogue with a partner.
3 Present your dialogue to the class.

PRONUNCIATION

4 🔊 **3.09 Listen and pay attention to the pronunciation of the *v* in *have to*. Check (✓) the sound you hear.**

have to
We **have to** buy him a present.
○ /f/ ○ /v/

5 🔊 **3.09 Listen again and repeat.**

 YOUR DIGITAL PORTFOLIO

Record your dialogue and upload it to your class digital portfolio.

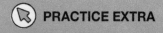 **PRACTICE EXTRA**

4 WE CAN SAVE OUR PLANET

 UNIT GOALS

- Talk about ways of protecting the environment.
- Read an infographic about the home of the future.
- Listen to a talk about being vegetarian.
- Learn about haikus.
- Write a reply to a comment on a blog about climate change.

 THINK!

1 Look at the image. What is its message?
2 What are some environmental problems in your area?

 VIDEO
4.1

1 Say two effects of global warming.
2 What gas do plants breathe in?

41

VOCABULARY IN CONTEXT

THE ENVIRONMENT

1 🔊 **4.01** Complete the posters with the words/phrases below. Then listen, check, and repeat the words/phrases.

- cut down
- destroy
- pollute
- protect
- ~~recycle~~
- reduce
- reuse
- throw away
- turn off
- waste

¹ _____Recycle_____ **your trash. Everybody's doing it.**

**Think of our future.
Don't** ² _____
the trees!

³ _____ **the lights.
Don't** ⁴ _____
energy.

Be part of the solution, not part of the pollution! Bike more, ⁵ _____ less.

**Don't feed the fish
on plastic.** ⁶ _____
our rivers and oceans!

Free our planet!
⁷ _____ **the use of
plastic.**

**There's no Planet B.
Don't** ⁸ _____ **the
environment!**

Don't ⁹ _____ **things
you can** ¹⁰ _____
another day!

2 Circle the correct options.

1 We *pollute* / (*recycle*) most of the trash in our house.
2 My sisters never *waste* / *turn off* the light when they leave their bedroom.
3 Mr. Kim wanted to *cut down* / *reduce* a tree in his yard, but he changed his mind.
4 People can *reduce* / *reuse* plastic bottles in different ways.
5 Hey, don't *pollute* / *throw away* that box! I can use it for an art project.
6 The school started a campaign to *destroy* / *protect* the life in the local river.

3 Complete the newspaper headlines with the correct form of the words/phrases below. There are two extra words/phrases.

- cut down • destroy • pollute • protect • recycle • reduce

1
TESTS CONFIRM: CHEMICAL COMPANY
_____ GREENVILLE RIVER

2
Mayor Robbins: "Factories
must not _____ the life
in our river!"

3
Company president promises
to _____ Greenville
River pollution to zero

4
" _____ our river!"
is the slogan of Greenville Middle
School eco movement

4 Complete the chart with the actions below.

- ~~cut down forests~~
- destroy the environment
- pollute the air
- protect wild animals
- recycle trash
- reduce CO_2 in the atmosphere
- reuse paper
- throw away batteries
- turn off electronic devices
- waste energy

Good For The Environment	Bad For The Environment
	cut down forests

 USE IT!

5 Work in groups of three. Write slogans for the posters.

READING

We all know we need to take action now so that we still have a planet in the future. And we can start at home! According to experts, houses in the next decades will be greener and more efficient. Check out some features:

A Houses will have a **"living wall"** – a wall covered with plants. If a living wall is 20 m², it converts 46 kg of carbon dioxide into oxygen per year! If you have a living wall in your house, you will help to clean the air.

B A living wall will also work as a **vegetable garden** to supply fresh, healthy food for the kitchen.

C Houses will have a **water tank** to **collect rainwater for the garden and the toilets.** If people use less water from the public water system, they will save money and help the local ecosystem.

D **Garages** will **provide electricity for the family car** – in fact, experts predict that 57% of cars will be electric in 2040. If this really happens, we will have much less air pollution.

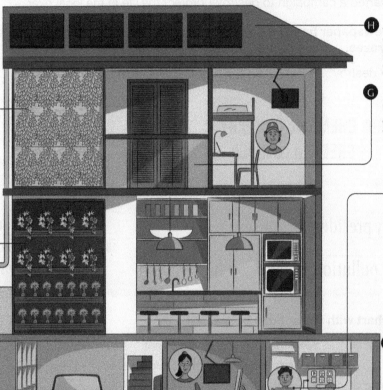

H All the **energy** will come from **solar panels on the roof** of the house.

G People will use **recycled wood and glass** to build their houses.

F People will **control the whole house from their smartphones or tablets.** And if you forget to turn off a light, sensors will do it for you!

E We will use more electricity than today because **many people will work from home.** This new lifestyle will demand **office spaces** at home with **the latest technology.**

---

1 **Look at the infographic. Check (✓) the best title.**

1 ○ Advantages and Disadvantages of Electric Cars

2 ○ How to Grow Plants in Your Garden

3 ○ This is How Your "Green" House Will Look in 2040!

2  4.02 **Read and listen to the infographic. Match 1–8 with sections A–H.**

People living in houses in 2040 will …

1 produce their own electricity. _A_

2 store water from the rain. _____

3 grow things to eat. _____

4 have a computer system to control the house. _____

5 have office spaces to work in. _____

6 reuse materials for building. _____

7 probably use electricity for driving. _____

8 have plants on the walls. _____

3 **Read the infographic again. Write _T_ (true) or _F_ (false).**

1 We can change our habits to save resources. _T_

2 We'll use new materials to build greener houses. _____

3 Houses will help save water and money. _____

4 In the future, people will not work at home. _____

5 People will be able to turn off their lights from anywhere in the world. _____

 THINK!

What feature of the house in the infographic do you like best? Can you think of any disadvantages of living in this house?

 WORKBOOK p.127

LANGUAGE IN CONTEXT

1 **Look at the examples below. Complete the sentences from the infographic.**

Zero Conditional	
If Clause (If + Simple Present)	**Result Clause (Simple Present)**
If a living wall [1] ___is___ 20 m²,	it [2] _____ 46 kg of carbon dioxide into oxygen.
If the air **becomes** polluted,	it **has** serious effects on people's health.

First Conditional	
If Clause (If + Simple Present)	**Result Clause (will/won't + Infinitive)**
If you [3] _____ to turn off a light,	sensors [4] _____ that for you!
If people [5] _____ less water,	they [6] _____ money.
If people **drive** electric cars,	we **won't need** so much oil.

2 **Write zero conditional sentences using the verbs in parentheses.**

1   plants (not have) water – they (die)

   ___If plants don't have water, they die.___

2   I (go) shopping – I (not use) plastic bags

   ----

3   my grandpa (visit) us on Sundays – he (not use) his car

   ----

4   it (rain) a lot – our water tank (collect) 50 liters of water

   ----

5   a house (have) solar panels – it (produce) its own energy

   ----

6   we (buy) water bottles – we always (recycle) them

   ----

3 **Complete the first conditional sentences with the correct form of the verbs below.**

• be   • ~~buy~~   • cut down   • not be   • ride   • work

1   If my aunt _____buys_____ an electric car, she will need electricity in her garage.
2   There will be less traffic on the roads if more people _____ from home in the future.
3   If Lucas leaves home early, he _____ late for school.
4   If people _____ bikes to school and work, they will reduce transportation costs.
5   Cities _____ cleaner if everyone recycles their trash.
6   If our neighbor _____ that big tree on our street, my mother will plant a new one.

 USE IT!

4 **Complete the first conditional sentences with your own ideas.**

1   If I live in a "green" house in 2040, --
2   I'll be happy in 2040 if --
3   If I don't have much homework tomorrow, --
4   I'll -- if it doesn't rain on the weekend.

5 **Work in pairs. Take turns sharing your ideas from Exercise 4.**

> If I live in a "green" house in 2040, I'll grow my own vegetables What about you?

> I'll have a water tank to collect rainwater.

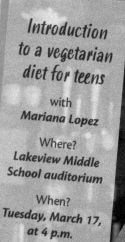

LISTENING AND VOCABULARY

1 Read the pamphlet about a talk at a school. Answer the questions.

1 What is the talk about?

---

2 Who will give the talk?

---

3 Who will probably go to the talk?

Introduction to a vegetarian diet for teens

with **Mariana Lopez**

Where?
Lakeview Middle School auditorium

When?
Tuesday, March 17, at 4 p.m.

2 Work in pairs. What do you know about being vegetarian? Write notes.

---

3 🔊 4.03 Listen to Mariana's talk. Does she mention any of your ideas from Exercise 2?

4 🔊 4.03 Listen again. Check (✓) the ideas you hear in Mariana's talk.

1 ✓ Mariana became a vegetarian to protect the environment.
2 ◯ Keeping cows, pigs, and chickens uses a lot of resources.
3 ◯ Vegetarians sometimes need extra vitamins in their diet.
4 ◯ Vegetarian meals are cheap and simple to make.
5 ◯ People who become vegetarians will probably enjoy their new diet.
6 ◯ Mariana's parents didn't want her to become a vegetarian.

5 🔊 4.04 Complete the sentences from the talk with the words below. Then listen, check, and repeat the phrases in bold.

- about   • in   • of   • ~~on~~   • to   • with

1 The environment and the future of our planet **depend** _____on_____ reducing the use of animal products.
2 I **worry** _____ climate change.
3 You should **pay attention** _____ what you eat.
4 If you **succeed** _____ making this change, I think you'll soon enjoy your vegetarian diet.
5 We need to **take care** _____ our planet.
6 At first, your meat-loving friends and parents might not **agree** _____ you.

✏️ **WORKBOOK** p.125

LANGUAGE IN CONTEXT

1 **Complete the sentences from Mariana's talk in the chart. Use the words below.**

• may find   • might need   • might not agree

	May and Might for Possibility
Affirmative (+)	You ¹_____ it hard to stop eating animal products. You ²_____ extra vitamins. Mariana **might discuss** vegetarian recipes in another talk.
Negative (–)	The restaurant **may not offer** vegetarian dishes on its menu. Your meat-loving friends and parents ³_____ with you.

2 **Complete dialogues with *may (not)*, *might (not)*, and the verbs.**

1 Liz   In the future, students will have classes online at home.
  Hank   I'm not sure about that. They _____ (want) to be away from their classmates.

2 Yuki   I'm going to the park this afternoon. Do you want to come?
  Sara   Hmm … I _____ (need) to help my grandpa after school. I'll send you a message, OK?

3 Nick   Vegetarians _____ (get) enough vitamins in their food.
  Ava   Yeah, they have to pay attention to what they eat.

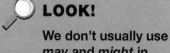 **LOOK!**

We don't usually use *may* and *might* in questions. We can form questions using *Is it possible that …?* or *Do you think …?*.

Is it possible that people will stop eating meat in the future?

3 **Rewrite the sentences using the words in parentheses (*may* or *might*).**

1 There's a chance Mariana will cancel her talk today. (may)

   ----

2 Perhaps my parents will buy electric bikes. (might)

   ----

3 Maybe this store doesn't open on Sundays. (might)

   ----

4 It's possible that people won't eat so much meat in the future. (may)

 USE IT!

4 **Complete the sentences with your own ideas.**

1 I might (not) _____
2 Our school may (not) _____
3 My friends might (not) _____
4 The world may (not) _____

5 **Work in pairs. Share your ideas from Exercise 4 and ask your partner questions.**

I might study in another country next year.

Really? Where?

ACROSS THE CURRICULUM

LITERATURE

Poetry and the Environment: HAIKUS

*I*nvented by the Japanese, haikus became popular in the western world in the 20th century. Nowadays people all over the world read, write, and love these short but powerful poems.

Haikus have three lines, but their organization is not so simple. Traditional haikus must have exactly 17 syllables, like this:

- line 1 – five syllables
- line 2 – seven syllables
- line 3 – five syllables

They are usually about nature and combine powerful images in a few words, to connect to one of our five senses: sight, sound, smell, taste, and touch. Haikus often have a *kigo* – a word or phrase that has a connection with a period of the year. Look at the English translation of two classic haikus by Matsuo Basho:

MEET BASHO, THE HAIKU MASTER

*M*atsuo Basho (1644–1694) was a samurai in his early days, but spent most of his life traveling around Japan, writing and teaching poetry. His haikus gained popularity all over Japan during his lifetime. He wrote about nature and the environment and expressed strong feelings through beautifully clear, simple images.

An old silent pond ...
A frog jumps into the pond,
Splash! Silence again.

None is traveling
Here along this way but I,
This autumn evening.

Modern haikus, however, don't always have such rigid structure, but are still organized into three lines. If you want to write a haiku, you don't need to worry about the number of syllables, but you may like to stick to nature themes.

Haikus for the environment

We asked our readers to send their haikus about the environment. Look at two poems we selected for this article (you can read all the haikus in our online magazine).

We cut down the trees
They sadly fell to the ground
Birds are silent now.

Julia, 15 – Brazil

Men burn ancient trees
Melt glaciers, raise oceans
There's no Planet B.

Santiago, 14 – Colombia

1 **Look at the magazine article. Check (✓) the people who might read it.**

1 ◯ people who like poems
2 ◯ people interested in international news

2 🔊 **4.05 Read and listen to the article. What is a haiku? Check (✓) the correct answer.**

1 ◯ a short poem   2 ◯ a poem about Japan   3 ◯ a Japanese poet

3 **Read the first part of the article again. Complete the sentences with the words/phrases below. There is one extra word/phrase.**

• after 1901   • complicated   • Japanese   • modern   • season   • theme   • three lines

1 Haikus became popular in western countries ___after 1901___.
2 Traditionally haikus are short, but that doesn't mean they're not _____.
3 Haikus only have _____, but their message is powerful.
4 Traditional haikus may have a word or phrase connected to a _____.
5 _____ haikus might have more than 17 syllables.
6 Nature is an important _____ in most haikus.

4 **Read the information about Matsuo Basho again. Check (✓) the sentence that is not correct.**

1 ◯ When he was young, Matsuo Basho was a samurai.
2 ◯ Basho's poems became famous after his death.
3 ◯ Basho taught and wrote poems while he was traveling around Japan.

5 **Read the last part of the article again. Do the teenagers' haikus have the same structure as traditional haikus? Work with a partner to count the syllables.**

WORDS IN CONTEXT

6 **Match the words with the images.**

1 pond _____
2 splash _____
3 melt _____
4 glacier _____

a
b
c
d

THINK!

Which of the four haikus in the article do you like best? What other poems do you like?

🔍 **WEBQUEST**

Learn more! Check (✓) True or False.
The theme of the World Children's Haiku Contest in 2019–2020 was animals.

◯ True   ◯ False

▶ **VIDEO**
4.2

1 What animals did the artists paint in caves in France?

2 What is the sculpture in the video made of?

WRITING

1 🔊 **4.06 Read and listen to an online comment about the infographic on page 44. Does it express a positive or negative opinion about it?**

SkepticalTeen

I think that this house of the future is a joke! In my opinion, there's nothing we can do, as individuals, to stop climate change. I strongly believe that governments and politicians should take action, not teenagers like us.

15 comments | Premium Member   👍 LIKE   ➢ REPLY

2 🔊 **4.07 Now read and listen to a reply to the comment. Does the writer agree with the comment?**

GreenGirl

I don't agree with SkepticalTeen at all! I loved the infographic about the house of the future, and many of the ideas presented in it are already available – they're just too expensive for our houses at the moment! I'd say that most people might not live in that type of house in 2040, but there's so much more we can do now! I'm certain that we can all find the time and energy to do some of the things below:

• Recycle plastic bottles.
• Turn off lights and save energy.
• Reuse things instead of throwing them away.

It's our responsibility to take action to help save our planet. If we don't act, we won't have a planet to save.

27 comments | Premium Member   👍 LIKE   ➢ REPLY

3 **Read the reply again and put a–e in the correct order 1–5.**

a conclusion _____

b opinion about the infographic _____

c examples of suggested actions _____

d opinion about the comment _____

e suggested actions _____

4 **Write a reply to SkepticalTeen's comment.**

1 Consider your opinion about SkepticalTeen's comment and the house in the infographic.

2 Think about possible actions governments, politicians, and teenagers can take to protect the environment.

3 Find or draw an image for your avatar and choose a username.

4 Write the first version of your reply. Use vocabulary from Unit 4.

5 **Switch your reply with a classmate and check his/her work. Use the checklist below.**

○ avatar and username

○ opinions about the comment and the infographic

○ actions people can take to protect the environment

○ conclusion

○ *may/might*

○ *zero/first conditional*

LOOK!

When we express opinions, we can use different phrases to make it clear how we feel about the topic.

• Strong opinion → *I strongly believe that … / I'm certain that …*

• Less strong opinion → *I think that … I'd say (that) …*

YOUR DIGITAL PORTFOLIO

Edit your reply, then publish it. Upload it to the class portfolio for everyone to see!

REVIEW
UNITS 3 AND 4

≡ VOCABULARY

1 Complete the descriptions in the boxes with advertising words. Use the letters below.

~~E~~ ~~T~~ R O ~~A~~ ~~T~~ ~~I~~ ~~M~~ H M R ~~S~~ D C P ~~E~~ O E U ~~I~~ ~~T~~ U ~~V~~ N C ~~D~~ I T R G ~~E~~ D S T A L O P D S A E R E A E R A E ~~N~~ ~~T~~ S P L O

A

an ¹ _advertisement_ to
² _____
consumers to buy something

B

a creative
³ _____
to ⁴ _____
consumers' attention

C

a description of the
⁵ _____

Ding-dong!
Who's at the door?

Organic fruit and vegetables from local farmers.
You choose what you want and when you want it.
We'll bring it directly to your door.

HealthInABox4U (312) 679-5678
www.healthinaboxforyou.com

D

something that
the company
⁶ _____ to do

E

a stylish ⁷ _____

2 Complete the sentences with the words/phrases below.

• ~~cost~~   • invest   • label   • on sale   • own   • sell

1 These secondhand clothes are good value: they _____cost_____ less than new ones from
   a famous _____.
2 I _____ a few gadgets, but my favorite ones are my headphones.
3 This T-shirt is too expensive. I'll wait until it's _____.
4 They _____ their jewelry in the local markets.
5 I'm going to _____ some money in my friend's company.

3 Write the opposites of verbs 1–5.

1 clean   p _o_ _l_ _l_ u _t_ _e_
2 plant   ___ u ___ d ___ ___ ___
3 protect   ___ ___ s ___ ___ ___ y

4 recycle   ___ h ___ ___ ___   ___ w ___ ___
5 save   w ___ ___ ___ ___

4 Make expressions with a word from each box. Then replace the words/phrases in bold in sentences 1–5
with the expressions.

| • ~~agree~~   • depend   • pay attention |
| • take care   • worry |

| • about   • of   • on |
| • to   • ~~with~~ |

1 I **have the same opinion as** Francisco. _____agree with_____
2 All of us should **protect** the environment. _____
3 Do you **think about the problems of** the planet? _____
4 **Listen carefully to** the speaker and you'll understand. _____
5 I **need the support of** my parents for money. _____

LANGUAGE IN CONTEXT

5 Complete the sentences with the words below.

- doesn't have to   • has to   • have to   • must   • must not

1 My father _____ has to _____ fly to the US tomorrow for an interview.

2 Gisela's parents insist on some rules in their house. For example, Gisela _____ turn off the lights when she leaves her bedroom. And she _____ be on the Internet for more than two hours a day.

3 Philip _____ wake up early tomorrow, so he's going to watch the late movie before going to bed.

4 Do you _____ get a visa to travel to another country?

6 Write zero and first conditional sentences with the correct form of the prompts and *if*.

1 fish / die – they / not have / enough oxygen / in their water (zero)

----

2 we / turn off / the lights – we / save / electricity (zero)

----

3 you / read / this book – you / know / how to make a cake (first)

----

4 people / not buy / this product – the company / not reduce / the price (first)

----

7 Complete the sentences using words/phrases from both boxes below.

- don't have to   • have to   • may   • might   • must not

- be   • drive   • see   • stop   • use

1 You _must not use_ cell phones.

4 You _____ so slowly now.

2 You _____ here.

5 The road _____ dangerous on a rainy day.

3 You _____ cows on the road.

LEARN TO LEARN

Make a sticky note dictionary

Write new vocabulary on sticky notes. On the other side, write translations of the words.

Read the note, say its translation, and check.

The Environment

recycle   pollute
reuse
protect   reduce

CHECK YOUR PROGRESS

I CAN...

- talk about ads and money   ☺ ○   ☹ ○

- use *have to, don't have to, must,* and *must not*   ☺ ○   ☹ ○

- talk about the environment   ☺ ○   ☹ ○

- use the zero and first conditionals, and *may* and *might*.   ☺ ○   ☹ ○

5

MY ONLINE SELF

UNIT GOALS

- Talk about what you see and do on the Internet
- Read different opinions on a debate site
- Listen to an informal talk about digital footprints
- Learn about teenagers' use of social media
- Express different points of view

THINK!

1 Do you think the image represents the girl's online life or offline life?

2 What three words would you use to describe your online life? And your offline life?

VIDEO

1 What is the most important effect of being online all the time?

2 Where can you find sidewalks with "smartphone lanes"?

53

VOCABULARY IN CONTEXT

STRONG ADJECTIVES

1 🔊 **5.01 Complete the headlines with the words below. Then listen, repeat, and check the words.**

- brilliant
- ~~crazy~~
- freezing
- huge
- shocking
- silly
- spectacular
- ugly
- useless
- weird

LinkSocial your social media   34,657 followers

Man breaks his own record
You'd have to be
1 _c r a z y_
to do this!

👍 ↪ ⤳

Brr! It's 2 _____
out there!

◀ Emergency services have to work in difficult conditions

Talking toothbrushes!

A 3 _____ invention 👎
or a 4 _____ 👍 product?

Nature

10 5 _____ **things that science can't explain**

1 Mystery in European forests: no one understands what causes these lights to appear every year.

Fruit&Veg4allofus
@Fruit&Veg4allofus

6 _____ vegetables shouldn't go to waste

Fruit & veggies don't have to be perfect. #stopwaste #uglyfruitishealthyfruit

2 days ago

★ ☆ ☆ ☆ ☆

Bad acting and a 7 _____ **story**

Don't waste your time watching this movie

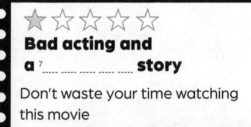

NEWS

8 _____ hurricane hits US coast!

9 _____ scenes! Volcano destroys thousands of homes

10 _____ **journeys in South America**
Discover the continent's amazing natural beauty

2 Complete the charts with the words in Exercise 1.

	Same Meaning
1 very strange	*weird*
2 very large	
3 insane	
4 of no use	
5 very surprising	
6 very intelligent	
7 very cold	

	Opposite Meaning
8 pretty	
9 smart	
10 dull	

LOOK!

Large means *big*.
I have a **large** dog, but my cousin has a small one.

3 Complete the chart with the words in Exercise 1. Add one more adjective in each column. Use a dictionary if necessary.

Positive Opinion	Negative Opinion	No Opinion
brilliant		

 USE IT!

4 Write three different adjectives from Exercise 3 to describe the use of technology in images 1–3.

1 _____   2 _____   3 _____

5 Work in small groups. Discuss your opinion of the use of technology in the images in Exercise 4.

I think using a laptop underwater a brilliant idea.

 Me too.

Really? I think it's silly.

READING

WHAT DO YOU THINK?
Join the debate

SHOULD SCHOOLS ALLOW CELL PHONES IN THE CLASSROOM?

? Around the world, more and more teenagers have cell phones and use them often. Cell phones can bring excellent learning opportunities, but they can also cause problems. Some countries (for example, France, Israel, and parts of China) don't allow any use of phones while students are at school, but this debate is very much alive.
Posted by: **Marion Smith**

Eduardo Morales, 2 days ago

I'm a high school teacher. Students wouldn't be able to concentrate if they had phones in the classroom: they would check their social media all the time. Some people say that cell phones can make it easier for students to share information and ideas in class, but I think that's ridiculous! Teenagers already spend too much time on their phones: if we allowed cell phones in class, students would spend even less time in face-to-face interactions. It's important to learn to work with people, not with electronic screens. Allowing cell phones in class is a crazy idea. If it was a good idea, most schools would allow them.

Sophie Graham, 1 day ago

I'm a principal. But before that I'm a teacher. I know a cell phone can bring huge benefits for students: they can use their phones as calculators and cameras, they can go on the Internet to look for information, read news stories, or use a dictionary. However, studies show that most students use cell phones in class to do other things not related to schoolwork. That's why we don't allow them in our school. If students didn't spend time texting and playing games, I wouldn't be against cell phones in class.

1 **Look at the text. Check (✓) the correct answers.**

1 Where is the text published?
   a ◯ in a high school blog
   b ◯ in a magazine about technology
   c ◯ on a website for discussing ideas

2 What is the text about?
   a ◯ opinions about using cell phones in class
   b ◯ advantages of having cell phones in schools
   c ◯ about how students use cell phones at school

2 🔊 **5.02 Read and listen to the text. Check (✓) the correct answers.**

1 Marion thinks that using cell phones in class ...
   a ◯ is a good idea.   b ◯ is a bad idea.   c ◉ can be both good and bad.

2 French schools ... the use of cell phones in class.
   a ◯ prohibit   b ◯ support   c ◯ don't have rules about

3 In ..., students must not use cell phones.
   a ◯ Eduardo's school   b ◯ Sophie's school   c ◯ Eduardo and Sophie's schools

4 ... doesn't see anything positive in allowing students to use phones in class.
   a ◯ Marion   b ◯ Eduardo   c ◯ Sophie

3 **Read Eduardo's comment again and answer the questions.**

1 Underline the argument Eduardo disagrees with.   2 Circle Eduardo's opinion of the argument.

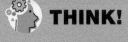

THINK!

In your opinion, should schools allow students to use cell phones in the classroom? Why / Why not?

        WORKBOOK p.131

LANGUAGE IN CONTEXT

1 Look at the examples below. Complete the sentences from the opinion website.

Second Conditional	
If Clause (If + Simple Past)	**Result Clause (would/wouldn't + Infinitive)**
If it ¹ _____was_____ a good idea,	most schools ² _____ cell phones.
If we ³ _____ cell phones in class,	students ⁴ _____ less time in face-to-face interactions.
If students ⁵ _____ time texting and playing games,	I ⁶ _____ against cell phones in class.
Questions (?)	
If you **had** the money, **would** you **buy** a new cell phone every year? How **would** you **feel** if your friend **stopped** speaking to you?	

2 Underline the simple past verbs and circle *would/wouldn't* + infinitive in 1–6 and a–f. Then match the two parts of the sentences.

1 If I <u>had</u> a camera, ___c___
2 If you wrote blog posts, _____
3 Your friends (would be) happier _____
4 What would you do _____
5 If the students didn't have a break between lessons, _____
6 If you were a parent, _____

a if they spent less time watching videos.
b they wouldn't be able to concentrate in class.
c I would become a vlogger.
d if people wrote bad comments about you online?
e would you allow your teenage child to have a debit card?
f I'm sure they would be brilliant.

3 Complete the sentences with the correct form of the verbs in parentheses.

1 If I _____had_____ (have) more time, I would take singing lessons.
2 If I _____ (know) how to cook, I would make healthy snacks and sell them.
3 If we _____ (not throw away) so much stuff, there would be less pollution.
4 _____ you _____ (live) abroad if you had a chance?
5 Your collage _____ (look) nicer if you _____ (add) some black and white images.
6 I don't have a smartphone, but if I _____ (have) one, I _____ (not use) it to buy things.

> 🔍 **LOOK!**
>
> To talk about unreal conditions, we use *would/wouldn't* (not *will/won't*).
>
> If I had more time, **I would learn** to play the piano.

 USE IT!

4 Work in pairs. Take turns asking and answering questions using the second conditional. Use the ideas below or your own ideas.

- be/fashion designer
- have/airplane
- live/abroad
- own/skatepark
- speak/five languages

💬 Where would you work if you were a fashion designer?

💬 I'd have my own business and work for myself.

LISTENING AND VOCABULARY

1 🔊 **5.03 Label the icons with the words below. Then listen, check, and repeat.**

- download • file • ~~password~~ • post • search • screenshot • tweet • upload

1 2 3 4

5 6 7 8

1 _password_   5 ....
2 ....   6 ....
3 ....   7 ....
4 ....   8 ....

2 **Look at the image and answer the questions with your predictions.**

1 Who is the young woman wearing glasses?
....
....

2 Where is she?
....
....

3 Why is she there?
....
....

3 🔊 **5.04 Listen, check, and correct your answers to Exercise 2.**

4 🔊 **5.04 Listen again and complete the diagram with notes about the main ideas. Compare your notes with a partner.**

1 What is it?	DIGITAL FOOTPRINT	2 How do we produce it?
------------------------ ------------------------ ------------------------		------------------------ ------------------------ ------------------------

3 Do we all have one?
○ Yes ○ No

5 **Write _T_ (true) or _F_ (false).**

1 We always leave a digital footprint when we "like" something online. ___T___

2 Strong passwords avoid digital footprints. _____

3 People can take images of chats that stay online for only seconds and post them in different places. _____

4 Hannah didn't get a job because of her digital footprint. _____

5 None of the students are surprised by Hannah's talk. _____

6 It is possible to change our digital footprint. _____

📝 **WORKBOOK** p.129

LANGUAGE IN CONTEXT

1 Complete the sentences from Hannah's talk in the chart. Use the words below.

- anyone
- anything
- nothing
- ~~someone~~
- something
- somewhere

Indefinite Pronouns		
Affirmative (+)	**Negative (–)**	**Questions (?)**
¹ ___Someone___ in the company searched for my name online.	There isn't **anyone** here who has a vlog. **No one** can have total privacy on the Internet.	Does ⁵ _____ know what "digital footprint" means?
When you search for ² _____, you always leave a trace.	You can't keep **anything** private when you go online. ⁴ _____ gives you complete protection.	Is there ⁶ _____ we can do to avoid problems?
They can post the screenshot ³ _____ else.	I can't find my file **anywhere**. My file is **nowhere** on this computer.	Did you go **anywhere** interesting last weekend?

2 Circle the correct options. What do the circled words describe? Write *T* (thing), *PE* (person), or *PL* (places).

1 Logan   Look! There's *anyone / someone* behind the tree. ___PE___
  Patricio   Where? I can't see *anyone / someone*. _____
2 Mariana How about going to the mall? I need to buy *something / anything* for Helen. _____
  Kathy   OK. I don't need to buy *something / anything*, but I'll go with you. _____
  Mariana Great. Let's go by bike then.
  Kathy   Hmm … I'm not sure. There's *somewhere / nowhere* to leave our bikes at the mall. _____
3 Jorge   Is there *anything / nothing* new on this channel? _____
  Karla   Yes. There's *something / nothing* about the history of social media. Do you want to watch it? _____
  Jorge   OK. Where's the remote control? I don't see it.
  Karla   It's *anywhere / somewhere* near that chair. _____

3 Complete the poster using words with *some–* or *any–*.

THINGS TO REMEMBER ABOUT ONLINE ACTIVITY

✓ Don't share your passwords with¹ ___anyone___.

✓ If you see ² _____ online that makes you uncomfortable, tell an adult.

✓ Use different passwords, change them often, and store them ³ _____ safe.

✓ If ⁴ _____ makes a comment you don't like about you, ask them to delete it.

✓ Don't write your address or phone number ⁵ _____ on social media.

✓ Don't share ⁶ _____ private that you receive from your friends without their permission.

 USE IT!

4 Work in small groups. Ask and answer questions about the advice in the poster in Exercise 3.

> Do you share your passwords with anyone?

about me   posts   contact me

Taking a Break from Social Media

Fernando Alves, Brazil

Until last month, I never paid too much attention to comments like "Teenagers are always on social media!" or "Too much time on social media can make you depressed." But then we had a school project: to find some facts about how Brazilian teens use the Internet and to compare the results to our habits. Here's a summary of what I discovered.

Facts	Comparison
82% of 9–17-year-olds are on social media.	My class: 100%
Brazilian teens check their social media 63 times a day on average.	Me: 71 times
Over half of teenagers in a study in Brazil said they almost always had a smartphone or tablet with them during meals.	My class: 80%

The project made me think: did I use social media too much? Did I feel anxious if no one liked my posts immediately? And I wondered: how would I feel if I didn't use social media for five days? So that's exactly what I did.

Day 1   I woke up and went straight to my phone. It was weird: no social media! ___b___

Day 2   I'm still anxious: did my friends like the photos I posted the day before yesterday? But I'm trying to keep busy with other things. _____

Day 3   Stress levels are lower. I texted some friends and enjoyed the one-to-one conversations. _____

Day 4   I spent my free time exercising and hanging out with my friends at the park. I left my phone at home. _____

Day 5   I decided to close some social media accounts and keep just two. I'll try to open them just two or three times a day in the future. _____

1 Look at the blog post. Check (✓) the options that describe what's in the post.

1 ◯ an introduction explaining why Fernando became interested in the topic
2 ◯ a diary describing Fernando's actions and feelings
3 ◯ advice that Fernando gives to other teenagers
4 ◯ the results of research Fernando did
5 ◯ recommendations about the best social media sites for teens

2 🔊 5.05 Read the blog post. Write a–e in the post to complete Fernando's diary entries. Then read, listen, and check.

a I think I'll feel happier that way.
b ~~During the day, I felt disconnected.~~
c It felt personal.
d I realized I don't depend on it to keep me happy.
e In fact, this evening I learned how to make sushi!

WORDS IN CONTEXT

3 Complete the sentences with the words below. Check your answers in the blog post.

- account   • average   • summary   • wonder

1 This is not the full text: it's just a _____ with the main ideas.
2 I spend 15–25 hours a week on homework – that's 20 hours on _____.
3 It's getting dark. I _____ what time it is. Do you know?
4 I can't persuade my cousin in the US to open an _____ on social media. He hates the idea.

4 Read the facts in the chart in the blog post and answer the questions. Then discuss your answers in pairs.

1 Did you know about these facts before reading the blog post?

----

2 Which is the most surprising fact in your opinion?

----

3 Do you have your phone with you during meals?

WEBQUEST

Learn more! Check (✓) the correct answer.
The logo of a famous social media site is a blue (or white) bird. What's the bird's name?

◯ **Tweet**   ◯ **Larry**   ◯ **Jack**

THINK!

Why do you think there may be a link between social media and depression? What can you do to avoid negative effects from social media?

VIDEO
5.2

1 How many internet users were there in July 2020?
2 What are trolls?

SPEAKING

EXPRESSING DIFFERENT POINTS OF VIEW

1 🔊 **5.06 Read and listen to a family at breakfast. What are three of the four people doing?**

Mother	Breakfast's ready! Phones down, please.
Son	Why do we have to put our phones down? Dad's on his computer.
Father	I'm working.
Daughter	And we're talking to our friends.
Father	I know, but that's not the same. I have something urgent to do.
Son	Sure, but I need to post this comment.
Daughter	Yeah, and my friends are important, too.
Mother	You know, that's a really good point, but it's family time now. Two minutes. And then ... no one uses a phone or computer!

2 **Circle the correct options.**

1 The son *agrees / disagrees* with his mother.
2 The father *agrees / disagrees* with his daughter.
3 The son *explains / doesn't explain* his point of view.
4 The daughter *agrees / disagrees* with her brother.
5 The mother *presents / doesn't present* a new point of view.

LIVING ENGLISH

3 **Complete the chart with the expressions below.**

- I know, but ... • Sure, but ... • Yeah, and ...
- You know, that's a really good point, but ...

1 I agree with you, but I want to make a different point.	....
2 That's true, but I don't think it's an important point.	....
3 I agree with you, and I want to make another point.	....

4 🔊 **5.07 Listen, check, and repeat the expressions.**

PRONUNCIATION

5 🔊 **5.08 Listen and pay attention to the pronunciation of the *o* in *something* and *wonder*.**

/ʌ/

I have s**o**mething urgent to do.
I w**o**nder why we have to put our phones down.

6 🔊 **5.08 Listen again and repeat.**

7 🔊 **5.09 Circle the letters in bold that have the same sound as the *o* in *something* and *wonder*. Then listen and check.**

1 a M**a**tch the columns.   b They don't have m**u**ch.
2 a S**o**me ads are smart.   b I feel the s**a**me way.
3 a C**u**t the carrots.   b She is c**u**te.
4 a I can r**u**n fast.   b I r**a**n to school.
5 a I'll leave s**oo**n.   b Who's your s**o**n?

8 🔊 **5.06 Listen to the dialogue again. Then practice with three classmates.**

9 **Role play a new dialogue. Follow the steps.**

1 Change the words in blue to write a new dialogue in your notebook.
2 Practice your dialogue with your classmates.
3 Present your dialogue to the class.

YOUR DIGITAL PORTFOLIO

Record your dialogue and upload it to your class digital portfolio.

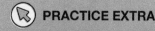 **PRACTICE EXTRA**

6

THE WORLD OF
MUSIC

UNIT GOALS

- Talk about different types of music and musical instruments.
- Read an online review about a band.
- Listen to an interview with a songwriter.
- Learn about the early history of hip-hop.
- Write two song reviews.

THINK!

1 Where are the people? How do you think they are feeling?

2 How important is music to you?

VIDEO

1 Who is Evelyn Glennie?

2 What happened to her when she was 12?

VOCABULARY IN CONTEXT

TYPES OF MUSIC

1 Look at the diagram. Check (✓) its objective.

a ◯ to show the best type of music for students at school

b ◯ to show students' favorite types of music in a school

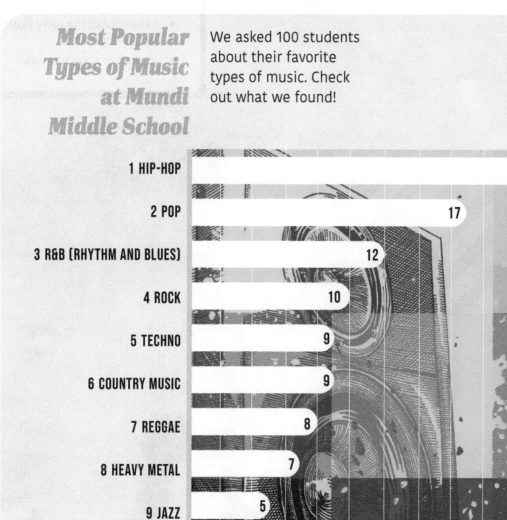

Most Popular Types of Music at Mundi Middle School

We asked 100 students about their favorite types of music. Check out what we found!

1 HIP-HOP	21
2 POP	17
3 R&B (RHYTHM AND BLUES)	12
4 ROCK	10
5 TECHNO	9
6 COUNTRY MUSIC	9
7 REGGAE	8
8 HEAVY METAL	7
9 JAZZ	5
10 CLASSICAL MUSIC	2

2 ◁ᴗ 6.01 Listen to ten music extracts. Match a–j with the types of music 1–10 in the diagram.

a   6
b   ....
c   ....
d   ....
e   ....

f   ....
g   ....
h   ....
i   ....
j   ....

3 ◁ᴗ 6.02 Listen, check, and repeat the types of music.

4 Label the images from music videos with the types of music below. There is one extra type.

- ~~classical music~~   • country music   • hip-hop   • jazz   • reggae   • rock   • techno

classical music

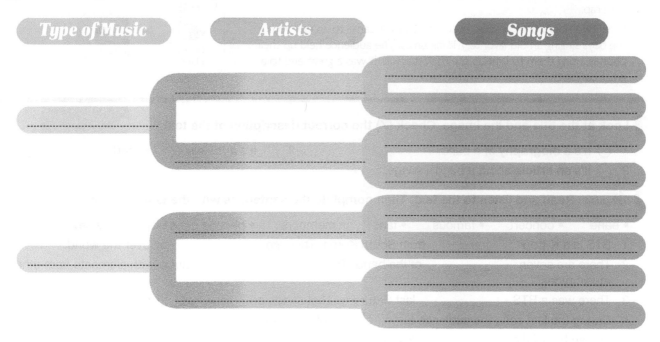

5 Write two types of music that you like in the chart. Then add your favorite artists and songs.

Type of Music   *Artists*   *Songs*

 USE IT!

6 Work in small groups. Use the chart in Exercise 5 to talk about your favorite types of music, artists, and songs.

My favorite type of music is pop and I really like Ed Sheeran.

Me too!

Well, he's OK, but I prefer hip-hop.

READING

Home | Music | Pop | Concert reviews

BTS Rocks Green Alliance Arena for a Memorable Night!

Leticia Harris | September 30 | ⏱ 3 min read

If you don't know the guys in the photo, they are the South Korean band BTS, the most popular Korean pop (or K-pop) group in the world. The seven bandmates have attracted millions of fans from Bangkok to Brazil. Their music is basically pop, but it has always included elements of hip-hop and rock.

I've seen some great concerts, but the one I went to last Saturday was one of the best. BTS didn't disappoint their devoted fans at the Green Alliance Arena. More than 55 thousand teenagers (and some parents) sang and danced to the band's greatest hits. It was an unforgettable concert.

The boys first went onstage to sing the most popular song from their recent album and then sang hits from previous ones. Their performance of ballads was amazing – Jungkook, V, Jimin, and Jin showed all their vocal power. After that, it was RM, Suga, and J-Hope's turn to show their talent with rap.

After two hours of incredible music, the concert came to an end with the boys singing an old favorite, *Mikrokosmos*. The audience held up their phones, using them to light up the dark stadium. It was a great end to a great concert!

3 comments

BTS Dad — *I was one of the parents at the concert last Saturday with my daughter. I've never been a fan of K-pop, but BTS is great!*

JaneT — *My son has never been to a concert. There's another BTS concert this Friday. Will it be safe for him to go with his friends?*

Leticia Harris — *It's safe! But tickets have sold out. Sorry!*

---

1 Look at the title and the image. Check (✓) the correct description of the text.

1 ○ It's a **biography** of a band.

2 ○ It's an **article** about a band's songs.

3 ○ It's a **review** of a concert.

2 🔊 6.03 Read and listen to the text. Then complete the sentences with the words below.

- band • concert • famous • fans • members • phones • pop • review

1 BTS is a K-pop _____band_____ from South Korea. They are _____ all over the world.

2 There are seven _____ of the band. They sing _____ music with elements from other music types.

3 There was a BTS _____ last Saturday. Thousands of _____ were there.

4 During the last song the audience turned on the lights on their _____.

5 The author of the _____ loved the concert.

3 Read the three comments again and answer the questions.

Who …

1 didn't expect to enjoy the concert? _____

2 is feeling anxious about a concert? _____

3 probably won't be able to go to the concert on Friday? _____

 THINK!

Why do you think JaneT is worried about her son going to a big music concert? How would you reply to her?

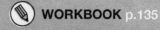 **WORKBOOK** p.135

LANGUAGE IN CONTEXT

1 Look at the examples below. Complete the sentences from the review.

Present Perfect: Affirmative and Negative	
Affirmative (+)	**Negative (–)**
I ¹_____'ve seen_____ some great concerts.	I haven't performed onstage. I ⁴_____ **never** _____ a fan of K-pop.
You **have listened** to this song a lot.	You **haven't met** my mom. You**'ve never heard** this band before.
She**'s downloaded** their new album. Their music ²_____ always _____ elements of hip-hop and rock.	JaneT **hasn't watched** any K-pop videos. My son ⁵_____ **never** _____ to a concert.
We**'ve learned** to read music at school.	We **haven't bought** tickets for the concert.
The seven bandmates ³_____ millions of fans.	They **haven't sung** this song very often.

2 Complete the sentences with the correct present perfect form of the verbs in parentheses.

1 The singers _____have performed_____ (perform) in different countries.
2 I _____ (not play) the piano in a concert.
3 Mike _____ (learn) to play six different instruments.
4 My mom _____ (not listen) to K-pop.
5 Erica _____ (meet) her favorite R & B singer.
6 Our band _____ (never appear) in public.

3 Complete the text with the correct present perfect form of the verbs below.

• buy   • never meet   • never watch   • say   • ~~see~~   • win

Beyoncé is my favorite R & B singer. I ¹_____'ve seen_____ her onstage three times, and she's a great performer. She's coming to my city again next week and I ²_____ a ticket for her concert. But my friend Liz ³_____ a radio competition and she's going to spend an afternoon with Beyoncé! She ⁴_____ the R & B diva, of course, and she's really excited about it. The funny thing is that Liz ⁵_____ a live concert and her parents ⁶_____ they won't let her go to Beyoncé's!

LOOK!

If we say when the action happened, we use the simple past, not the present perfect.

She **has seen** that movie. (= at some time in the past)

She **saw** it **last Saturday**.

USE IT!

4 Look at the list. Check (✓) the things you've done.

○ go to a live concert   ○ meet a famous person   ○ sing in public
○ listen to K-pop   ○ perform on a stage   ○ win a competition

5 Work in pairs and tell your partner what you have and haven't done from Exercise 4.

> I've been to a live concert.   Really? Who did you see?

LISTENING AND VOCABULARY

1 🔊 **6.04 Label the musical instruments with the words below. Then listen, check, and repeat.**

- drums
- guitar
- flute
- French horn
- keyboard
- saxophone
- trumpet
- ~~violin~~

1

.... violin ....

2

....

3

....

4

....

5

....

6

....

7

....

8

....

2 🔊 **6.05 Listen and write the name of the musical instruments you hear.**

1 .... drums ....
2 ....
3 ....
4 ....
5 ....
6 ....
7 ....
8 ....

3 🔊 **6.06 You're going to listen to a talk show with a songwriter. Which four instruments from Exercise 1 do you think she plays? Listen and check your predictions.**

1 ....
2 ....
3 ....
4 ....

4 🔊 **6.06 Listen to the talk show again. Number the questions in order (1–5).**

a Have you ever fallen in love? ....
b How many songs have you written? ....
c Was it about a specific person? ....
d Has music always been important in your life? ....
e What instruments do you play? ....

5 Circle the correct options.

1 Kate Queen was *14 / 16* when she wrote her first song.
2 Her *friends' / parents'* relationships inspired Kate to write her first song.
3 Kate wrote her first song using her *guitar / keyboard*.
4 A lot of her *dance / love* songs have been number one.
5 She has written *more / less* than 100 songs.

✏️ **WORKBOOK** p.133

LANGUAGE IN CONTEXT

1 Complete the questions and answers from the talk show in the chart. Use the words below.

- be   • ~~fall~~   • write

Present Perfect: Questions and Short Answers		
Yes/No Questions (?)	[1]____Have____ you ever ____fallen____ in love? [2]_____ music always _____ important in your life? **Have** many people **heard** Kate's songs?	Yes, I [3]_____. / No, I **haven't**. Yes, it [4]_____. / No, it **hasn't**. Yes, they **have**. / No, they **haven't**.
Wh– Questions (?)	How many songs [5]_____ you _____? What **has** Kate **done** recently? How **have** her songs **influenced** other musicians?	

2 Put the words in order to make questions. Then match the questions with the answers.

1 have / where / recently / Marina and Ana / been ?

_____Where have Marina and Ana been recently?_____ ____d____

2 you / for the concert / tickets / bought / have ?

_____ _____

3 Jake / how many times / seen / has / Kate onstage ?

_____ _____

4 my saxophone / have / ever / you / I / shown ?

_____ _____

5 Kate / has / an interview / why / given ?

_____ _____

a Only once or twice, I think.
b Because her fans want to know more about her.
c Yes, I have. I used my debit card.

d To their grandma's house in the country.
e No, you haven't. Can I see it?

 USE IT!

3 Work in pairs. Take turns asking and answering questions with *Have you ever ...?* using the verbs below.

- eat   • go to   • have   • listen to   • watch   • travel

> Have you ever traveled by plane?

> No, I haven't. What about you?

by plane

Indian food

a classical music concert

a talk show

jazz

guitar lessons

MUSIC

The Early History of HIP-HOP

Hip-hop is a cultural movement that started in the 1970s, in African-American and Latino neighborhoods in New York. Its main art form is rap music, but hip-hop also involves DJing, graffiti painting, and breakdancing. Rapping – speaking words rapidly in rhythm – is the way hip-hop artists perform most of their songs. Check out some important events in the movement in the 20th century.

1973 "The father of hip-hop," *DJ Kool Herc*, aged 16, DJs a party for his sister's birthday in the Bronx, a poor neighborhood in New York.

1977 Hip-Hop spreads outside poor areas, with rappers performing all over New York.

1979 Sugarhill Gang records the first commercial hip-hop song, *Rapper's Delight*.

1981 A national news magazine program reports the "rap movement" for the first time.

1982 Hip-Hop arrives in Hollywood! *Wild Style* is the first movie to show hip-hop and graffiti artists.

1986 Run-DMC, a famous hip-hop group, records *Walk This Way*, a classic from rock band Aerosmith. Run-DMC is the first hip-hop group to be nominated for a Grammy.

1990 Hip-hop hits the popular TV screen with *The Fresh Prince of Bel-Air*, a series starring Will Smith.

1992 Artists from California start to dominate the hip-hop scene. Dr. Dre, one of the most famous West Coast rappers, records his first solo album.

1998 Jay-Z and Eminem release albums and increase the popularity of hip-hop.

1999 Singer Lauryn Hill's album *The Miseducation Of Lauryn Hill* is the first hip-hop album to be Album Of The Year at the Grammy Awards.

2000 Hip-hop is the most popular type of music in the United States and a global phenomenon.

1 Look at the organization of the article and complete the sentence with the words/phrases below. There are two extra words/phrases.

- a conclusion   • alphabetical   • an introduction   • chronological

The article has a paragraph as ¹_____ and then the information is presented in ²_____ order.

2 🔊 6.07 Read and listen to the article. Write *T* (true) or *F* (false).

1 Hip-hop is a cultural movement that includes different art forms. __T__
2 Rapping is the way hip-hop artists sing and play musical instruments. _____
3 Before 1979, there weren't any commercial recordings of hip-hop songs. _____
4 In 1986, Aerosmith recorded Run-DMC's song. _____
5 In the 1990s, Dr. Dre, Jay-Z, and Eminem become famous hip-hop artists. _____

3 Read the article again and answer the questions.

1 Who is "the father of hip-hop"?

_____DJ Kool Herc is "the father of hip-hop"._____

2 When did Sugarhill Gang record *Rapper's Delight*?

----

3 What was the first movie to show hip-hop?

----

4 Which TV series brought hip-hop to a wider audience?

----

5 Who was the first hip-hop artist to get a Grammy for Album Of The Year?

----

6 When did hip-hop become the most popular type of music in the US?

WORDS IN CONTEXT

4 Match the expressions from the article with their definitions.

1 spread _____   a make a recording available to the public to buy
2 nominated _____   b reach a wider area
3 release _____   c prize
4 award _____   d included in a competition for a prize

 WEBQUEST

Learn more! Check (✓) the correct answer.
In hip-hop concerts, the MC is the person who performs the rap. What is the original meaning of "MC"?

○ Master of Charts
○ Mic Controller
○ Master of Ceremonies

 THINK!

How popular are hip-hop and hip-hop artists in your country? What's your opinion of this type of music?

 VIDEO
6.2

1 What is *Schuhplattler*?
2 Where is it from?

WRITING

1 🔊 **6.08 Read and listen to the reviews. Check (✓) what they are about.**

a ⚪ songs   b ⚪ concerts   c ⚪ movies

● ● ●   _ ☐ ✕

Somewhere Over the Rainbow

Singer: Judy Garland
Year of recording: 1939

Judy Garland sang *Somewhere Over the Rainbow* in the 1939 movie *The Wizard of Oz*. She played the role of Dorothy in the movie when she was only 16 years old. Garland sang  it with the orchestra of the movie studio, which was usual in musicals at that time. The performance and the beautiful lyrics about hope and optimism make *Somewhere Over the Rainbow* one of the greatest songs of the 20th century. Hundreds of other artists have recorded the song.

Cover singer: Ariana Grande

Year of cover recording: 2017

Ariana Grande sang *Somewhere Over the Rainbow* for the first time in the *One Love Manchester* charity concert in England, in June 2017, 11 days after  her earlier concert in Manchester ended in tragedy. Her performance is very emotional and includes elements from jazz, with just a keyboard as a musical instrument. The song has had millions of downloads and has raised millions of dollars for charity.

---

2 **Read the reviews again. Write *JG* for Judy Garland and *AG* for Ariana Grande.**

1 She recorded the song in the 21st century. __AG__

2 She recorded the song for a movie. _____

3 There were a lot of musicians in the recording of her song. _____

4 She performed the song in a live concert. _____

5 People have donated a lot of money in order to listen to her song. _____

3 **Write a review of a famous song and a review of its cover version.**

1 Choose an original song that has a cover version and listen to the songs.

2 Collect information about the original song and its cover version.

3 Find or draw images of the two singers.

4 Write the first version of your reviews. Use vocabulary from Unit 6.

4 **Switch your reviews with a classmate and check his/her work. Use the checklist below.**

⚪ an original song and its cover version

⚪ information about the artists and when/where the recordings took place

⚪ images of the singers

⚪ opinions about the style and feeling of each performance

⚪ verbs in the present perfect

 LOOK!

In a song review, we usually include facts about the artist(s) and when/where the song was recorded. We also give opinions about the style and feeling of the performance.

 YOUR DIGITAL PORTFOLIO

Edit your review, then publish it. Upload it to the class portfolio for everyone to see!

REVIEW
UNITS 5 AND 6

💬 VOCABULARY

1 **Circle the correct options.**

1 Brr! It's difficult to get up early for school when the weather is *crazy* / (*freezing*)

2 Marie Curie was a *brilliant* / *silly* scientist. She got two Nobel prizes.

3 The photos of Ben's accident were *shocking* / *useless*! I'm happy he's OK.

4 There are seven bedrooms at Sofia's house. It's a *huge* / *weird* place.

5 The view of the mountains from our hotel room was *spectacular* / *ugly*.

2 **Complete the sentences with the correct internet words.**

1 You can't d o w n l o a d a large f _ _ _ now. The internet connection is too slow at the moment.

2 I took a s _ _ _ _ _ _ _ _ _ of Santiago's last t _ _ _ before he deleted it from Twitter.

3 You don't need a username and p _ _ _ _ _ _ _ to s _ _ _ _ _ for information on that website.

4 To p _ _ _ your photos on the online album, first you need to u _ _ _ them to the website.

3 **Put the letters below in the correct order. Then match the words with the descriptions.**

- cork   - gargee   - ~~ohtnee~~   - sisccalal ciums   - veyha tamel

1 fast electronic dance music _____techno_____

2 popular music from Jamaica _____

3 began as rock and roll in the 1950s _____

4 Beethoven and Mozart played it _____

5 very loud rock music with electric guitars _____

4 **Can you guess the musical instruments? Label the images.**

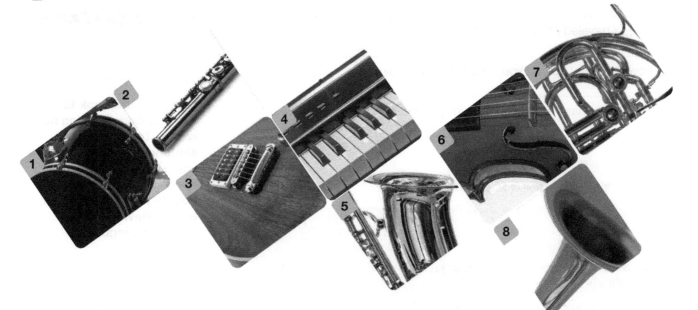

1 _____drums_____   5 _____

2 _____   6 _____

3 _____   7 _____

4 _____   8 _____

LANGUAGE IN CONTEXT

5 Complete the second conditional sentences with the correct form of the verbs in parentheses.

1 If Haru _____knew_____ (know) how to cook, he _____wouldn't eat_____ (not eat) so much junk food.
2 If the students _____ (have) tablets in class, they _____ (be) able to look for information.
3 If Bia _____ (buy) a new cell phone, she _____ (take) better photos.
4 Mateo _____ (not go) to the movies tonight if he _____ (need) to study.
5 I _____ (not be) happy if I _____ (not listen) to music every day.

6 Complete the dialogue with the words below.

• anything   • ~~anywhere~~   • no one   • someone   • something   • somewhere

Hailey   Have you seen my phone? I can't find it ¹___anywhere___.
Diego   No, I don't know where it is.
Hailey   Well, I'm sure I left it ²_____ in this room. I think ³_____ has taken it.
Diego   Don't be silly. There's ⁴_____ here except me and I don't have it.
Hailey   Well, where is it, then? This is terrible. I can't do ⁵_____ if I don't have a phone.
Diego   Wait a minute – there's ⁶_____ in your pocket. What's that?
Hailey   Oh! It's my phone. Great! Thanks, Diego.

7 Complete the sentences with the correct present perfect form of the verbs below.

• buy   • not have   • never listen   • perform   • ~~sing~~

1 Mariela is a great singer. She _____has sung_____ in public many times.
2 I _____ tickets for the hip-hop festival on Saturday.
3 My sister _____ lessons, but she plays the guitar really well.
4 Our band _____ on stage three times.
5 My best friend loves jazz, but I _____ to that type of music.

8 Put the words in the correct order to write questions.

1 you / a / seen / live / you / have / concert / ever ?
----

2 times / traveled / how / by / have / many / plane / you ?
----

3 how / money / spent / you / much / today / have ?
----

4 family / in / has / ever / your / country / lived / another ?

LEARN TO LEARN

Writing new words in example sentences

Use your notebook to write sentences using new words. Try to make the sentences meaningful to you – they can be about personal experiences or people who are important to you. Review your sentences regularly.

I started learning to play the flute when I was 11.

When we use the school computers, we can't download anything.

CHECK YOUR PROGRESS

I CAN...

• describe things with strong adjectives and talk about the Internet   ☺ ○ ☹ ○

• use the second conditional and indefinite pronouns   ☺ ○ ☹ ○

• talk about different types of music and musical instruments   ☺ ○ ☹ ○

• use the present perfect for experiences.   ☺ ○ ☹ ○

7

AFRICA: PAST, PRESENT, AND FUTURE

⊙ UNIT GOALS

- Talk about achievements.
- Read an article about African innovation.
- Listen to a podcast about a movie.
- Learn about the Himba people of Namibia.
- Present new information.

🧠 THINK!

1 When you think of Africa, what facts and images do you think of?

2 Look at the pages in this unit quickly. Do the topics and images match your ideas? Do they give you other ideas?

▶ VIDEO
7.1

1 How many countries are there in Africa?

2 How many languages do people speak in Africa?

ACHIEVEMENTS

1 🔊 **7.01** Circle the correct options to complete the fact file. Then listen and check.

GREAT CIVILIZATIONS OF ANCIENT AFRICA

THE CITY OF CARTHAGE was the center of an important empire until the 2nd century BCE. It was famous for the ¹*produce / production* of a purple pigment of great value. Wars with Rome destroyed the city, and most of the ruins we can see today are Roman buildings.

THE ANCIENT EGYPTIANS are famous for their ²*achieves / achievements*, including the ³*develop / development* of a complex writing system called hieroglyphics. No one knew how to read it until the ⁴*discover / discovery* of the Rosetta Stone in the 18th century.

THE MALI EMPIRE was one of Africa's greatest civilizations. King Mansa Musa (1280–1337), the richest person the world has ever seen, used his money to ⁵*construct / construction* amazing buildings in Timbuktu.

THE PEOPLE OF AKSUM (also called Axum) ⁶*organized / organization* commerce between Africa and India, and their empire had great influence until the 7th century. Some of the huge obelisks they built still ⁷*survive / survival* today.

ATLANTIC OCEAN

INDIAN OCEAN

2 🔊 **7.02 Complete the charts. Then listen, check, and repeat.**

Verbs	Nouns Ending in –*ment*
1 achieve	.... *achievement* ....
2 develop	....

Verbs	Nouns Ending in –*tion*
4	construction
5	organization
6 produce	....

Verbs	Nouns Ending in –*y*
3 discover	....

Verbs	Nouns Ending in –*al*
7	survival

3 **Check (✓) the correct missing words in the sentences.**

1 The … of the Cape Town Stadium took almost three years.
  a ◯ achievement   b ⊘ construction   c ◯ survival
2 Kenyan runners have … great success in the Olympic Games.
  a ◯ achieved   b ◯ discovered   c ◯ organized
3 The … of gold in the late 19th century brought thousands of people to South Africa from all over the world.
  a ◯ organization   b ◯ development   c ◯ discovery
4 Factories use robots for the … of cars.
  a ◯ achievement   b ◯ production   c ◯ survival
5 To …, pandas need to eat 12–38 kg of bamboo every day.
  a ◯ survive   b ◯ achieve   c ◯ organize
6 Albert Sabin …. the oral polio vaccine in the 1950s.
  a ◯ organized   b ◯ constructed   c ◯ developed

🗣 USE IT!

4 **Complete the chart using your own ideas.**

Something you've achieved this year	....
A discovery you've made recently	....
An organization you belong to	....
Something that's necessary for your survival	....
The most important item your country produces	....

5 **Work in pairs. Take turns asking and answering questions about your information and your partner's information.**

What have you achieved this year?

I've learned how to write a rap.

When did you do that?

1 Look at the title, headings, and images in the article. Circle the correct options in the sentence below.

The article is about *technological inventions / survival techniques* that some people *have developed / might develop* in a *country / continent*.

LOOKING FOR INNOVATION? HERE'S AFRICA FOR YOU

A large and young population that wants change. Countries like Rwanda and Ethiopia, examples of the world's fastest growing economies. Many problems to solve. These ingredients make Africa the perfect place for innovation. In fact, some recent African developments have already surprised the world.

SMART GLOVES FOR SIGN LANGUAGE

Roy Allela's niece was born deaf and has to use sign language. Because no one in Allela's family could communicate with her, he designed a translation glove: his niece wears the glove and connects it to a phone. The phone then translates her hand movements into an audio message. Allela's dream is to see these gloves in all Kenyan schools that have deaf students. He hasn't achieved this objective yet, but he's working hard on it.

3-D PRINTERS FROM E-WASTE

Electronic waste from around the world is one of Africa's big problems. Afate Gnikou from Togo has decided to do something with it: he has constructed 3-D printers using parts of old computers, scanners, and other electronics. He now works with a lab which has given these printers to local schools. In the future, Gnikou wants to use these printers to make medical equipment to help disabled people.

WATER FROM THE AIR

There is six times more water in the air than in all the rivers on Earth. During a drought in 2016, when Kenya had almost no rain, Beth Koigi had a brilliant idea: her Majik Water invention uses a chemical process to take water from the air and convert it into drinking water. She has already produced a prototype of her invention.

2 🔊 7.03 Read and listen to the article. What motivated these people to create something? Write *A* (Allela), *G* (Gnikou), or *K* (Koigi). There is one extra answer.

1 a problem with old objects ....
2 money difficulties ....
3 a problem in the family ....
4 extreme weather conditions ....

3 Write *T* (true) or *F* (false).

1 The article lists three reasons to explain why there are many innovations in Africa. ....T....
2 Allela's invention produces a written message on a phone screen. ....
3 For his 3-D printer Gnikou uses materials that people have thrown away. ....
4 Students near the lab Gnikou works with are making medical equipment with their printers. ....
5 Koigi's Majik Water produces cleaner drinking water from rivers. ....
6 The three inventors have done everything they wanted to achieve. ....

 THINK!

Each of these innovators invented something to solve a problem. What problems do you see around you and what inventions might help solve them?

 WORKBOOK p.139

LANGUAGE IN CONTEXT

1 **Look at the examples below. Complete the sentences from the article.**

Present Perfect with *Already*, *Just*, and *Yet*		
Already	*Just*	*Yet*
I **have already finished** my homework. Beth Koigi [1] .... a prototype. Some African developments [2] .... the world.	I know Felipe is at home. I**'ve just spoken** to him. It**'s just started** raining. Let's stay here. My brothers **have just gone** out. They left five minutes ago.	We **haven't uploaded** the file **yet**. Roy Allela [3] .... this objective .... **Have** you **met** my cousin **yet**? **Have** scientists **discovered** a cure **yet**?

2 **Put the words in the correct order to make sentences and a question.**

1 lives / invention / already / This / improved / our / has

   ~~This invention has already improved our lives.~~

2 have / posted / I / photos / some / online / just

   ----

3 haven't / The / the / downloaded / students / yet / file

   ----

4 We / the / events / organized / have / sports / already

   ----

5 yet / company / developed / Has / an / the / app ?

 LOOK!

Use *already* and *just* after *have/has*.

I **have just** received your email.

She **has already** written the summary.

3 **Tamara has to write a blog post about an African invention. Look at her checklist and write what she has and hasn't done. Use *already*, *just*, and *yet*.**

1   ~~She has already chosen the invention.~~

2   --

3   --

4   --

5   --

1 choose the invention ✓
2 search for information ✓
3 write the first draft ✓
4 ask a friend for feedback
5 produce the final version

 USE IT!

4 **Write sentences about yourself with *already*, *just*, and *yet* in your notebook. Use the ideas below or your own ideas.**

- do all my homework for tomorrow
- learn how to use *already*, *just*, and *yet*
- finish Exercise 3
- take driving lessons
- have lunch
- turn 15

5 **Work in groups. Take turns reading your sentences to the group. Discuss the sentences and then tell the class some information about your group.**

Adriana has already done all her homework for tomorrow.

Pedro and I haven't finished Exercise 3 yet.

LISTENING AND VOCABULARY

1 Look at the image of a man skimboarding.
Then work in pairs and discuss the answers to the questions.

1 Have you ever heard of skimboarding? Have you ever done it?
2 Do you think skimboarding is a cool thing to do? Why / Why not?

2 🔊 7.04 Listen to the beginning of a podcast. Match 1–4 with a–d.

1 The name of the podcast is ....   a a movie about a skimboarder.
2 Today's episode is about ....   b *Skimboarding Pro*.
3 The title of the movie is ....   c Dlamini Pod.
4 The director of the movie is ....   d Sofia Vieira.

3 🔊 7.05 Listen to the whole podcast and circle the correct options.

1 Sofia has made several movies about *Angola / surfing*.
2 Pedro spent a lot of time *watching the surfers / skateboarding near the beach*.
3 When he started skimboarding he *knew a lot / didn't know anything* about the sport.
4 In 2019 *a movie director / some sports people* saw that Pedro was good at skimboarding.
5 The movie has received *positive / negative* reviews.
6 The critic believes Sofia's movies are successful because she loves *Angola / telling stories*.

4 🔊 7.06 Complete the b sentences using a word from each box so that they mean the same as
the a sentences. Then listen, check, and repeat the phrases.

| • afraid | • famous | • good |
| • interested | • proud | • ~~tired~~ |

| • at | • for | • in |
| • ~~of~~ | • of | • of |

1 a Waiting for the bus always makes me feel impatient.

   b I'm _____ tired of _____ waiting for the bus.

2 a My brother sings well.

   b My brother is _____ singing.

3 a Everyone knows about Brazil's beaches.

   b Brazil is _____ its beaches.

4 a Spiders don't make me feel scared.

   b I'm not _____ spiders.

5 a I don't like kayaking anymore.

   b I'm not _____ kayaking anymore.

6 a My dad's paintings make him feel good about himself.

   b My dad is _____ his paintings.

 WORKBOOK p.137

LANGUAGE IN CONTEXT

1 Complete the sentences from the podcast in the chart. Use the words below and *since* or *for*.

- 's been ... a few weeks
- 's received ... the opening night
- 've been ... many years

Present Perfect with *Since* and *For*	
Since	**For**
I**'ve lived** in Angola **since 2021**. You**'ve studied** French **since February**. Sofia **has made** movies about Angola **since she left college**. It ¹_____ excellent reviews _____.	I ²_____ a big fan _____. You**'ve been** my English teacher **for a long time**. It ³_____ in movie theaters _____. We**'ve watched** TV **for two hours**.
How long have you known Marco? I've known him **since I was 11**. / I've known him **for four years**. **How long** has your sister played the guitar? **Since last year**. / **For ten months**.	

2 Complete the sentences with *for* or *since*.

1 My father has liked painting _____*since*_____ he was a teenager.
2 I've played the piano _____ I was six years old.
3 Here's a snack. You haven't eaten anything _____ hours!
4 My cousins have had a vlog _____ two years.
5 South Africa has been an independent country _____ 1910.
6 This company hasn't developed a new product _____ a long time.

 LOOK!

Use the present perfect with *since*.

I **have known** my best friend **since** I was five. (= We have been friends for ten years.)

3 Write questions with *how long* and answer the questions.

1 you / be / at this school? (since)

_____
_____

2 you / live / in your neighborhood? (for)

_____
_____

3 you / know / your best friend? (since)

_____
_____

4 your English teacher / be / in the classroom? (for)

_____
_____

 USE IT!

4 Check (✓) *Yes* or *No* so that the answer is true for you.

	Yes	No
Do you play a musical instrument?		
Do you have a pet?		
Are you interested in sports?		
Do you have a smartphone?		

Do you play a musical instrument?

Yes, I play the guitar.

How long have you played it?

5 Work in pairs. Take turns asking the questions in Exercise 4. When your partner answers *Yes*, find out more information by asking a question with *How long*.

The Himba

The Himba almost disappeared in the 1980s because of war and drought. Since then, their population has grown. People think there may be more than **25,000** Himba in Namibia today.

Good thinkers

The modern world hasn't had much influence on traditional Himba culture. That's why scientists are interested in studying the Himba. One of the questions scientists want to answer is: "Do the Himba think in the same way as people in other societies?" The results of some studies have shown that the Himba are better at finding creative ways to solve problems. Also, their attention to detail is amazing and they achieve better results on tests like the Ebbinghaus illusion than many other people.

The Ebbinghaus illusion: which orange circle is bigger?

Himba ways

In Himba society the men make political decisions and look after the cows and goats. The women milk the animals, carry water to the village, cook, and build their huts.

Himba women and men are famous for their complex hairstyles. Girls, women, older boys, and men all wear their hair in braids, but in different styles. Some young girls wear braids over their faces and older girls start wearing a headpiece made of goat skin, which looks like three leaves. After getting married or having a child, they wear a different headpiece. Himba women also cover their bodies with butterfat – the fat from cow's milk – and red coloring.

Tradition and modern life

Since Namibia's independence in 1990, some things have changed for the Himba. Some young people have already left their villages to get a job or go to school. Some haven't come back. In the villages, some Himba think integration with the modern world is necessary, while others think it will destroy their culture. Time will tell.

1 **Look at the text. Check (✓) the correct options.**

1 The text is from …
   a ◯ a story book for children.
   b ◯ an encyclopedia for young people.
   c ◯ a history textbook for teenagers.

2 The objective of the text is to …
   a ◯ tell a story about an African family.
   b ◯ explain how some African people lived in the past.
   c ◯ give information about an African society.

2 **7.07 Read and listen to the text. Check (✓) the false sentence.**

1 ◯ Most Himba people have kept their traditional culture.
2 ◯ In Himba society, hairstyles have important meanings.
3 ◯ Scientists have tested the way Himba people think.
4 ◯ The Himba population today is smaller than in the 1980s.

3 **Circle the correct options.**

1 In Himba society men and women *share /* (*don't share*) the same responsibilities.
2 Himba men don't have to *take care of animals / construct homes*.
3 Women change their *hairstyle / skin color* when they get married.
4 The Himba have shown that they can *develop illusion tests / think creatively*.
5 The Himba are *good at / proud of* concentrating on details.
6 *All / Not all* Himba who get a job come back to their village.

WORDS IN CONTEXT

4 **Find these words in the text and label the images.**

• goat   • hut   • leaves   • braids

  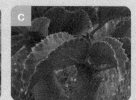 

------------------   ------------------   ------------------   ------------------

5 **In your notebook, write captions for images 1–5 in the text. Use the words in Exercise 4 and information from the text.**

THINK!

Think about an indigenous society you know (from Africa or from another continent). What are the people good at? What can they teach other societies?

WEBQUEST

Learn more! Check (✓) the correct answer.
Which orange circle is bigger in the Ebbinghaus illusion? What other illusions like this can you find?

◯ the circle on the left
◯ the circle on the right
◯ the circles are the same size

VIDEO

7.2

1 What's a djellaba and where do people wear them?
2 What is the name the fashion show that appears in the video?

SPEAKING

1 🔊 **7.08** **Read and listen to the vlog. Then match 1–3 with a–c.**

Rafaela Hi, I'm Rafaela and welcome to my music channel.
OK, so for a long time I've wanted to find a way to hear the best of new African music. And guess what? I've just found out that there's the perfect app – it's called Music&More. Basically, you choose the country or type of music you like. Then the app shows what teenagers around the world have listened to and liked recently. This is how it works …

1 The vlog is about _____
2 In Music&More you can select _____
3 The app shows _____

a "Nigeria" and "rap," for example.
b the music other teenagers have enjoyed.
c an app that introduces you to new music from Africa.

LIVING ENGLISH

2 **Complete the chart with the expressions below.**

- basically, … • guess what? • I've just found out …

Expression used to introduce …	
1 a summary of the main information	-------------------
2 something exciting	-------------------
3 information you've discovered recently	-------------------

3 🔊 **7.09** **Listen and repeat the expressions.**

PRONUNCIATION

4 🔊 **7.10** **Listen and pay attention to the different pronunciations of –ed.**

/t/ lik**ed**   /d/ listen**ed**   /ɪd/ want**ed**

5 🔊 **7.10** **Listen again and repeat.**

6 🔊 **7.11** **Listen and complete the chart with the correct words below.**

- decided • lived • played • posted • ~~searched~~ • walked

/t/	/d/	/ɪd/
searched		

7 🔊 **7.08** **Listen to the vlog again. Then take turns reading the vlog to a partner.**

8 **Role play a vlog about an app you've started using recently. Follow the steps.**

1 Decide on the topic of your app: music, food, movies, art, or sports.
2 Write the text for your vlog in your notebook. Use the vlog in Exercise 1 for ideas.
3 Take turns reading your vlog to a partner and comment on your partner's vlog.

YOUR DIGITAL PORTFOLIO

Record your dialogue, then upload it to your class digital portfolio.

🔍 PRACTICE EXTRA

8 WHAT'S IMPORTANT TO ME?

 UNIT GOALS

- Talk about things that are important to you.
- Read a pamphlet about a game.
- Listen to interviews about volunteer work.
- Learn about teenagers in the Netherlands.
- Write up an interview with a classmate.

 THINK!

1 In your opinion, what's the boy in the image thinking about?

2 How do you make decisions about things that are important in your life?

 VIDEO

8.1

1 What three sports are there in a triathlon?

2 Name three types of motivation in the video.

85

PHRASES WITH *DO*, *HAVE*, AND *MAKE*

1 Look at the images and read the labels. Then circle the correct options.

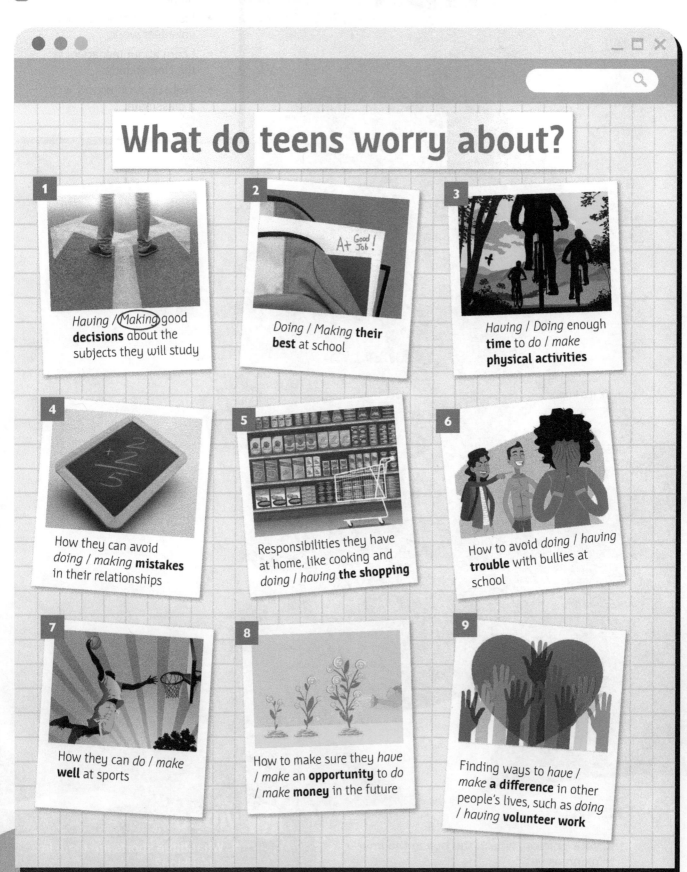

What do teens worry about?

1 *Having /* (*Making*) good **decisions** about the subjects they will study

2 *Doing / Making* **their best** at school

3 *Having / Doing* enough **time** to *do / make* **physical activities**

4 How they can avoid *doing / making* **mistakes** in their relationships

5 Responsibilities they have at home, like cooking and *doing / having* **the shopping**

6 How to avoid *doing / having* **trouble** with bullies at school

7 How they can *do / make* **well** at sports

8 How to make sure they *have / make* an **opportunity** to *do / make* **money** in the future

9 Finding ways to *have / make* **a difference** in other people's lives, such as *doing / having* **volunteer work**

2 🔊 **8.01 Complete the four descriptions with *do*, *have*, or *make* and the words below. Then listen, check, and repeat the phrases.**

- a difference   • the shopping   • ~~volunteer work~~

I ¹ _____do volunteer work_____ every week at our community center. I ² _____ for people who can't leave their homes. I want to ³ _____ in the world.

- an opportunity   • physical activities   • time

Studying is important to me. I don't ⁴ _____ very often – only in PE classes at school – and I don't ⁵ _____ to go out every weekend. But I know that if I focus on my goals, I'll ⁶ _____ to study abroad when I'm older.

- decisions   • trouble   • well

I'm a "study buddy" at school. When students ⁷ _____ with a school subject, they can come and talk to me. I also help them ⁸ _____ about which elective classes to take. I like to help other students to ⁹ _____ at school.

- mistakes   • money   • your best

I own an online channel about computer games, and I ¹⁰ _____ from it! I think it's important to ¹¹ _____ and I want to start my own game company one day. I'm learning a lot about the industry – even when I ¹² _____ , I learn something from them.

3 Write the phrases from Exercise 2 in the chart.

do	have	make
volunteer work		

USE IT!

4 Write answers to the questions using your own ideas.

1 Who do you talk to when you have trouble at home?

_____

_____

2 How important is it to you to make a lot of money in the future?

_____

_____

3 Have you ever done volunteer work? If so, where?

_____

_____

4 How can teenagers make a difference in the world?

_____

_____

5 Work in pairs. Take turns asking and answering the questions in Exercise 4.

DILEMMA TEENS

In this fun game, you and your friends try to suggest solutions to dilemmas that teens might face. Do you think you know your friends well? Play **Dilemma Teens** and find out!

Check out some dilemmas you will face in **Dilemma Teens!**

D1

Your best friend has had a jewelry business for a few months – she uses beads to make necklaces and bracelets. You have always thought her pieces are awful, but you have never said anything.

Yesterday, she asked you to write a review of her jewelry for her blog. You agreed to do it.

What do you do? Do you lie in your review?

D2

You did volunteer work at an animal shelter last year. Although you love animals, you decided to leave after six months because the coordinator always shouted at everyone.

She called you yesterday asking for help. All the other volunteers have stopped working there. She was very insistent on the phone.

What do you do? Do you go and help at the shelter?

D3

You're a "study buddy" at school. A student has had a lot of trouble with math and she didn't do well last semester. You helped her study for a math test, but she still made a lot of simple mistakes the day before.

The teacher gave the test scores yesterday and this student got an A. You think she cheated on the test.

What do you do? Do you tell the teacher?

You can play **Dilemma Teens** face-to-face or download the app and challenge your friends anywhere, anytime!

---

1 **Look at the pamphlet. Check (✓) its purpose.**

1 ◯ to advertise a game   2 ◯ to review a game   3 ◯ to give instructions for a game

2 🔊 **8.02 Read and listen to the pamphlet. Complete the sentences with the phrases below.**

- avoiding a difficult person   • being honest   • causing trouble
- keeping quiet   • taking care of animals   • ~~telling a lie~~

1 In card D1, the choice is between _____ *telling a lie* _____ and _____ about a friend's work.

2 In card D2, the choice is between _____ and _____.

3 In card D3, the choice is between _____ for someone and _____.

3 **Read the thoughts of four players. Match them with the dilemma cards. There is one extra thought.**

a "Hmm ... I can't stand people shouting at me, but the poor dogs and cats need help." _____

b "What a difficult situation! Why ever did I agree to do that?" _____

c "Gosh ... should I tell a lie about my bad grade? Or should I tell the truth?" _____

d "Well, the teacher trusts me, but I'm not completely sure she copied her answers from another student." _____

 THINK!

Work in pairs. Take turns answering the questions on the dilemma cards. Explain your suggested solutions.

  WORKBOOK p.143

LANGUAGE IN CONTEXT

1 Look at the examples below. Complete the sentences from the pamphlet.

Present Perfect vs. Simple Past	
Unspecified Time in the Past	Your best friend ¹ ___has had___ a jewelry business for a few months. You ² _____ always _____ her pieces are awful, but you ³ _____ never _____ anything. A student ⁴ _____ a lot of trouble with math.
Specific Time in the Past	**Yesterday**, she ⁵ _____ you to write a review of her jewelry for her blog. You ⁶ _____ volunteer work at an animal shelter **last year**. She ⁷ _____ well **last semester**.

2 Complete the sentences with the present perfect or simple past form of the verbs in parentheses.

1 This a great game! We ___have played___ (play) it a lot.
2 Alice and her sister _____ (start) their jewelry business when they were 13.
3 Juan and I _____ (not have) any trouble using the app on the weekend.
4 Martin is a math tutor at school. He _____ (help) a lot of students with their work.
5 The students _____ (never work) at an animal shelter before.

 LOOK!

If there is a word/phrase saying when the action happened, for example *yesterday*, *last week*, *two days ago*, we don't use the present perfect.

She called you **yesterday** asking for help.

3 Write sentences with the prompts about the inventor of Dilemma Teens.

Emily Lopez, inventor of **Dilemma Teens**, a game with moral dilemmas for teens

1 Emily / invent / the game when she was 15
___Emily invented the game when she was 15.___
2 her father / help / her sell the first version in 2019
_____
3 her game / be / in toy stores since 2020
_____
4 the game / already / sell / 25,000 copies
_____
5 Emily / create / an app for the game last year
_____

USE IT!

4 Write two true sentences and one false sentence about things you have done.

1 _____
2 _____
3 _____

I've met Cristiano Ronaldo.

5 Work in pairs. Take turns sharing your sentences from Exercise 4. Ask your partner questions to find out which sentence is false.

Really? Where did you meet him?

LISTENING AND VOCABULARY

1 🔊 **8.03 Look at the image. Check (✓) the sentence you think describes the situation better. Then listen and check.**

1 ◯ A college student is asking people some questions for a project.
2 ◯ A reporter is interviewing people about the traffic in the city.

2 🔊 **8.03 Listen again. Check (✓) the correct people in the chart.**

Who ...	Girl	Boy	Woman
1 has done volunteer work?	✓		
2 worries about poor people?			
3 has/had the influence of family members?			
4 works/worked with older people?			
5 lost a family member last year?			
6 definitely likes to read?			

3 🔊 **8.03 Listen once more. Write the correct sentences.**

1 The girl started doing volunteer work when she was 12.
   ~~The girl started doing volunteer work when she was 14.~~

2 People go to the food bank because they don't know how to cook.
   ----

3 The boy wrote letters for the residents at the retirement home.
   ----

4 The boy's grandmother had dementia.
   ----

5 The woman does volunteer work at a book club.
   ----

4 **Read the sentences from the interview and circle the correct options.**

1 I **work** (for) / to the local food bank.
2 They **fight** for / with everyone's right to education.
3 They really **care** about / to other people.
4 It's terrible to **suffer** at / from dementia.
5 It was difficult for me to **deal** for / with that.
6 I **belong** to / with a book club.

5 🔊 **8.04 Listen, check, and repeat the words in bold and the correct options in Exercise 4.**

✏️ **WORKBOOK** p.141

LANGUAGE IN CONTEXT

1 Complete the subject questions from the interview in the chart. Use the words below.

• happened   • inspired   • made

Subject Questions	Object Questions
Who **works** for a food bank?	What organization **does** the girl **work** for?
What organization **gives** food to people?	What **does** the food bank **give** to people?
Who **belongs** to a book club?	What club **do** you **belong** to?
Who ¹_____ you?	How **did** your parents **inspire** you?
What ²_____?	When **did** that **happen**?
What ³_____ you decide to do that?	What decision **did** you **make**?

2 Put the words in the correct order to make questions about the interview. Then match the questions with the answers.

1 Saturdays / the girl / on / where / go / does?
   _____*Where does the girl go on Saturdays?*_____   __d__

2 at / works / who / food bank / the ?
   _____   _____

3 gets / from / who / the food bank / help ?
   _____   _____

4 in / retirement home / lived / a / who ?
   _____   _____

5 the boy / what / do at the home / did ?
   _____   _____

6 ago / happened / year / a / what ?
   _____   _____

a He read to the residents.
b Volunteers.
c The boy's great-grandmother died.

d To the local food bank.
e The boy's great-grandmother.
f People who can't afford food.

 USE IT!

3 Write six quiz questions with the prompts in your notebook.

   _____*1 Who painted the Mona Lisa?*_____

1 Who / paint / the *Mona Lisa*?
2 Who / Juliet / fall in love with in Shakespeare's play?
3 What / destroy / Pompeii in 79 AD?
4 What colors / appear / on the South African flag?
5 When / the coronavirus pandemic / start / in China?
6 Which young girl / win / the Nobel Peace Prize in 2014?

4 Work in pairs. Take turns asking and answering the questions in Exercise 3. How many can you answer correctly?

GEOGRAPHY

Where Do the HAPPIEST Teenagers in the World Live?

The answer is they probably live in the Netherlands, a country in Europe that is famous for its tulips and windmills, and smaller than most states in Brazil. With 17 million people, the country has succeeded in giving its teen inhabitants an optimistic view of life that contrasts with other rich countries, such as the UK and the United States.

What is the secret of Dutch teens' happiness? As for any complex question, there are several answers.

▸ The Netherlands is a wealthy country that takes care of its young people. According to a report from UNICEF, 95% of Dutch children are happy with their lives.

▸ The Netherlands Institute of Social Research states that Dutch teens in general have positive relationships at home, at school, and with friends. Parents encourage their children to be independent and teachers are not authoritarian. Teenagers feel they can trust adults.

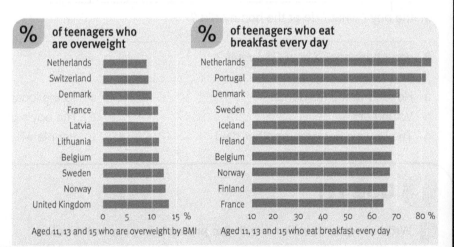

% of teenagers who are overweight

- Netherlands
- Switzerland
- Denmark
- France
- Latvia
- Lithuania
- Belgium
- Sweden
- Norway
- United Kingdom

0 5 10 15 %

Aged 11, 13 and 15 who are overweight by BMI

% of teenagers who eat breakfast every day

- Netherlands
- Portugal
- Denmark
- Sweden
- Iceland
- Ireland
- Belgium
- Norway
- Finland
- France

10 20 30 40 50 60 70 80 %

Aged 11, 13 and 15 who eat breakfast every day

▸ Dutch teens are generally healthy. Over 80% of them have breakfast every day and only 8% of the teen population are overweight. Most students ride their bikes to school every day (in fact, cycling is a normal form of transportation for people of all ages in the Netherlands).

▸ There is some bullying in Dutch schools, but according to studies, it doesn't happen as often as in other countries. 86% of Dutch teenagers say their classmates are helpful and kind.

▸ Although they have experienced more pressure from homework and exams in recent years, Dutch teens are still happy at school. One of the reasons is the school system, which allows high school students to change study programs or even repeat a year if they are not happy with their academic progress.

1 Look at the title of the article and the images. Check (✓) the article's main objective.

1 ◯ to give different opinions about happiness among Dutch teenagers
2 ◯ to give information about happiness among Dutch teenagers

2 🔊 **8.05** Read and listen to the article. Check (✓) the correct answers.

1 The Netherlands is … Brazil.
   a ◯ bigger than   b ◯ smaller than   c ◯ the same size as
2 In general, Dutch teenagers are … teenagers in the UK and in the US.
   a ◯ happier than   b ◯ unhappier than   c ◯ as happy as
3 Research shows that Dutch parents want their children to be … .
   a ◯ optimistic   b ◯ independent   c ◯ rich
4 Dutch teenagers have a lifestyle that is good for their … .
   a ◯ friends   b ◯ family   c ◯ health
5 Most teenagers in the Netherlands have a … image of their classmates.
   a ◯ positive   b ◯ negative   c ◯ neutral
6 When Dutch students choose their study program at school, they … change it later.
   a ◯ can   b ◯ can't   c ◯ must

3 Read the article again. Match the numbers below with the information a–e.

• 17   • 85   • 86   • 95

a percentage of Dutch teens who like the people they study with ＿＿＿
b percentage of teens in the Netherlands who always have a meal at the start of the day ＿＿＿
c percentage of children in the Netherlands that say they have a happy life ＿＿＿
d population of the Netherlands in millions ＿＿＿

WORDS IN CONTEXT

4 Match the words (1–4) with their definitions (a–d).

1 windmill ＿＿＿
2 wealthy ＿＿＿
3 state ＿＿＿
4 pressure ＿＿＿

a officially say or write
b a structure with parts that turn with the movement of the air
c sense of stressful urgency
d having a lot of money

WEBQUEST

Learn more! Check (✓)
T (true) or **F** (false).
There are more bicycles than
people in the Netherlands.

◯ True   ◯ False

THINK!

How happy do you think teenagers
are in your country? Think about
teenagers' attitudes to family, school,
and friends.

VIDEO
8.2

1 How many people around the world
   meditate?

2 What do you have to do to practice
   mindfulness or meditation?

WRITING

1 🔊 **8.06 Read and listen to an interview with a Dutch teenager. Check (✓) the topics mentioned in the interview.**

1 ◯ hobbies   2 ◯ friends   3 ◯ school   4 ◯ family

INTERVIEWS

Kenno Appelhof is 15 years old. He has friends, goes to school, and argues with his parents sometimes, as most teenagers do. He also lives in the Netherlands, one of the countries where teenagers are the happiest in the world.

WSM Kenno, what makes you happy?

Kenno Oh, so many things. My dog Buddy makes me happy, my friends make me laugh and are an important part of my life.

WSM Who gives you help if you need it?

Kenno My family and close friends. They're people that I can depend on.

WSM How do you like your school?

Kenno I love going to school and I know getting a good education is important for my future.

Most of my friends are from school, so that's where I see them every day.

WSM What's the most important thing in your life?

Kenno I love school and spending time with my friends, but the most important thing in my life is my family. They really support me and care about my happiness. It's great to know there are people you can always trust.

2 You're going to interview a classmate about what makes him/her happy and the important things in his/her life. Write four questions for your interview.

1 ....
2 ....
3 ....
4 ....

🔍 LOOK!

When we write up an interview, we organize it into questions and answers. We usually include a short introduction about the person interviewed.

3 Work in pairs. Take turns asking your partner your questions from Exercise 2. Take notes on his/her answers.

4 Write up the interview you did with your classmate.

1 Find or draw an image of the classmate you interviewed.
2 Write a short introduction about your classmate.
3 Write your questions and use your notes to write up your classmate's answers.
4 Write the first version of your interview. Use vocabulary from Unit 8.

5 Switch your write-up of the interview with your classmate and check each other's work. Use the checklist below.

◯ image of the person interviewed
◯ introduction about the person interviewed
◯ subject and object questions
◯ correct information in the answers

** YOUR DIGITAL PORTFOLIO**

Edit your interview, then publish it. Upload it to the class portfolio for everyone to see!

REVIEW
UNITS 7 AND 8

📄 VOCABULARY

1 Look at the underlined words and write *C* (correct) or *I* (incorrect). Write the correct words if necessary.

1 Mozambique was a Portuguese possession in Africa until the country <u>achievement</u> independence in 1975.
   I   achieved

2 The economic <u>development</u> of some countries in Africa depends on tourism. _____ _____

3 The <u>discover</u> of diamonds in the national park has attracted a lot of attention. _____ _____

4 Let's <u>organize</u> interviews with the volunteers for the animal shelter. _____ _____

5 We're worried about the <u>survive</u> of the wild animals in the forest. _____ _____

6 If they <u>construction</u> a road across the village, people will lose their houses. _____ _____

2 Complete the mini dialogues with the prepositions below.

- at   • ~~in~~   • for   • of (x 3)

1 A Are you interested _____in_____ joining the drama club?
   B Well, I'd love to, but I don't think I'm good _____ acting.

2 A Hey, you've been in this room since 3 p.m. Aren't you tired _____ studying?
   B I sure am, but I'm afraid _____ not doing well in the history test tomorrow.

3 A That city is famous _____ the beautiful sculptures in its parks.
   B Yes, and the people who live there are very proud _____ them.

3 Complete the text with *do*, *have*, or *make*.

Volunteering for young people

by Clara Santos

People who [1] _____do_____ volunteer work [2] _____ the opportunity to [3] _____ a difference in the world. There are a lot of things you can do.

I volunteer for an organization that helps people who can't leave home – I [4] _____ their shopping every week, for example. My brother and sister [5] _____ physical activities with the kids in our neighborhood.

Volunteers don't have a salary or [6] _____ money from their work, but volunteering is a serious thing. Be sure you [7] _____ time for the tasks you promise to do because other people are depending on you.

---

4 Circle the correct options.

1 My older sister has suffered (from) / *with* insomnia for some time.

2 Do you belong *for* / *to* any sports clubs at your school?

3 I can't stand selfish people who don't care *about* / *with* others.

4 Lucy is a part-time babysitter. She works *for* / *from* a family with six children!

5 Can the school counselor help students deal *to* / *with* emotional problems?

6 Many women around the world fight *for* / *to* equal pay for men and women.

5 Look at the images. Circle the sentence that describes each image.

a The game has already started.
b The game hasn't started yet.

a He has already finished breakfast.
b He hasn't finished breakfast yet.

a They have just left school.
b They haven't left school yet.

6 Write present perfect sentences with the verbs in parentheses and *since* or *for*.

1 I began to study classical music in 2020. (study – since)
    I have studied classical music since 2020.

2 We met Sayuri in July. It's December now. (know – for)

3 My sister has a vlog. She started it in January. (have – since)

4 The last time Luiza saw her grandparents was two weeks ago. (not see – for)

5 Mr. Harris is a math teacher. He began working as a teacher in 2019. (be – since)

7 Write questions with the prompts in the present perfect or the simple past.

1 you / ever / travel / to another country?

2 you / go / to the movies last weekend?

3 your English class / have / a test yesterday?

4 your classmates / already / eat / their lunch?

8 Write questions for the answers. Pay attention to the <u>underlined</u> words/phrases.

1 I talked with <u>Cathy</u> last night.

2 <u>A car accident</u> happened in front of our school.

3 <u>K-pop bands</u> made me decide to study Korean.

4 Lucas plays <u>five musical instruments</u>.

CHECK YOUR PROGRESS

 I CAN...

• talk about achievements and use adjectives with prepositions ☺ ● ☹ ●

• use the present perfect with *already, just, yet, since,* and *for* ☺ ● ☹ ●

• use expressions with *do, have,* and *make*, and verbs with prepositions ☺ ● ☹ ●

• understand the difference between the present perfect and the simple past, and ask subject and object questions. ☺ ● ☹ ●

LEARN TO LEARN

Listing collocations

Creating diagrams helps you see collocations (words/phrases that we often use with other words/phrases). Create diagrams of collocations in your notebook and use different colors (for example, blue for verbs and green for nouns). Also write examples using the collocations.

I always try to do my best.

GAME CHANGER EXTRAS

READING 1

ACROSS THE CURRICULUM / SCIENCE

A TEENAGE INVENTOR

1 **Look at the title and the images. Discuss the questions with a partner.**

1   Make a list of the things you did before 9 a.m. this morning. How many of those activities used electricity?

2   What do you think the teenager invented?

2 🔊 **R.01 Read and listen to the article. Were your ideas in Exercise 1 correct?**

An Inspirational Teenage Inventor

Hannah Herbst was nine years old when she started writing to Ruth, her penpal in Ethiopia. After four years of writing to each other, Hannah learned many things from Ruth. One of the things that surprised Hannah the most was that many people in Ethiopia lived with limited access to electricity and running water. Hannah, from the US, had access to electricity and water every day. It made her sad to hear that many people were living in this situation. She decided she wanted to invent something to help solve the problem of energy poverty, even though she didn't know much about engineering and she didn't have a strong interest in math or science.

When Hannah was thirteen years old she started designing a prototype called BEACON – *Bringing Electricity Access to Countries through Ocean Energy*. Inspired by the ocean where she lived in Florida, she had the idea to create electricity using the energy of the ocean currents and store it in a battery.

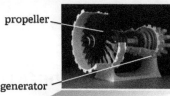
propeller
generator

Hannah didn't design the prototype alone, she had different mentors who helped her. The mentors taught her that often the best solutions are the simplest ones. Before making a final design, her mentors encouraged her to change the prototype and develop her ideas. Her mentors also encouraged her to share her ideas in competitions. That's when she entered the competition called the 3M Young Scientist Challenge, and won the title of America's Top Young Scientist in 2015. The invention created many opportunities for Hannah, such as presenting the idea to the US President at the White House.

Hannah graduated from Atlantic University in 2020 where she studied Information Systems and Business Analytics. She loves to inspire students to study math and science and try to come up with inventions to solve the world's difficult problems.

3 **Read the article again and answer the questions.**

1   Who did Hannah write to regularly when she was young?
----

2   What problem did Hannah want to solve? Why?
----

3   What challenges did Hannah face?
----

4   What did her mentors teach her?
----

5   What source of energy did BEACON use?
----

6   What does Hannah do now?
----

4 **Think about Hannah's journey to study computer engineering. Discuss the questions with a partner.**

1   How were Hannah and Ruth's lives different as teenagers?

2   What things helped Hannah become a scientist?

3   Is it possible for everyone to have the same opportunities in life? Is that OK?

 THINK!

Do you think young people can be good inventors? Why / Why not?

READING 2

AROUND THE WORLD

LJUBLJANA: GREEN CITY

1 Look at the images. Discuss the questions with a partner.

1   What problem and solution do the images show?   2   Why do you think Ljubljana is a "green" city?

2 ◀)) R.02 Read and listen to the report about Ljubljana. Were your ideas in Exercise 1 correct?

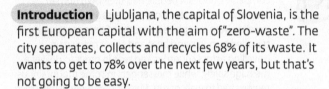

Name of city: Ljubljana
Country: Slovenia
Population of city: Over 288,000
Language: Slovene (or Slovenian)
Interesting fact: Ljubljana's aim is zero-waste

Introduction   Ljubljana, the capital of Slovenia, is the first European capital with the aim of "zero-waste". The city separates, collects and recycles 68% of its waste. It wants to get to 78% over the next few years, but that's not going to be easy.

Problem   Before 2004, most of the waste in Ljubljana went to a **landfill** or incinerators. The people of Ljubljana now produce only 115 kg of non-recyclable trash per person per year. That's amazing, but 115 kg of trash is still a problem. Why? We now know that burning or **burying** our trash creates health problems. It's also a terrible waste of our natural resources to use things just once and then throw them away.

Solution   So how did Ljubljana change in such a short time? The first step was to collect separated waste from **door to door**. People started to feel responsible for their waste and they began to separate it better.

If you separate used glass, cardboard, plastic, and organic trash, you can recycle them. But when you throw different kinds of trash away together, you create waste.

Ljubljana has **recycling bins** downtown and there are two waste recycling centers where people can take their trash. They also try to encourage people to reuse things that people throw away. At one of the recycling centers, they check, clean, **fix**, and sell things at low prices. And there are even classes to teach people how to fix broken things.

Conclusion   Ljubljana is a good example of a green city, because people recycle and reuse a lot of their trash. Creating cities that are zero waste is important because if we reuse and recycle trash, we can save money and protect the environment and people's health.

3 Read the text again. Write *T* (true) or *F* (false). Then circle the facts and underline the opinions.

1   Ljubljana has a population of over a quarter of a million people. T

2   It's difficult for a city to recycle 78% of its trash. _____

3   Burning our trash is a good idea. _____

4   You create waste by throwing different types of trash away together. _____

5   People in Ljubljana take their trash to the recycling centers. _____

4 Complete the sentences. Use the words/phrases in bold in the article.

1   The politician went from _door to door_ explaining the idea of "zero waste".

2   They couldn't _____ our old car, so we took it to the recycling center.

3   _____ trash in the ground causes environmental problems.

4   In the US, they send half of their trash to a _____.

5   Images on the _____ show people what they can throw away in each container.

THINK!

What things do you reuse instead of throwing them away? Why?

📖 READING 3

ACROSS THE CURRICULUM / HISTORY

THE HISTORY OF COMMUNICATION

1 Look at the title and the images. Discuss the questions with a partner.

1 How did people send messages to each other before the invention of the telegraph?

2 Why was communication limited before the invention of the telegraph?

2 🔊 **R.03** Read and listen to the infographic. Were your ideas in Exercise 1 correct?

HOW PEOPLE COMMUNICATED IN THE PAST

The way we communicate with each other now is very different from the early forms of communication. Sending a simple message could take many days or even weeks in the past.

Smoke Signals

Smoke signals are the oldest form of visual communication. The Chinese used them first in 200 BCE to send messages along the Great Wall of China. In 150 BCE, the Greeks also used smoke signals to represent the alphabet so they could send messages easily to each other. Later, many countries around the world used smoke from the top of a hill to signify danger. Simple but effective!

Carrier Pigeon

The Egyptians used pigeons for long-distance communication from the 12th century AD. The pigeons carried messages from Egypt to cities that were hundreds of kilometers away. Then the Romans and Greeks used pigeons, and later, many European countries used pigeons during World War I and World War II to send messages that helped save many people's lives.

Human Messengers

In the Middle Ages and before, cities, countries, companies, and rich people had their own human messengers to send important messages as quickly as possible from one place to another. Some messengers travelled by horse and boat and spent many days travelling across countries and seas in order to deliver a message safely, while messengers in some mountainous regions had to walk or run. Messengers were usually men who were fit and healthy. Sometimes it was a dangerous job and some messengers even worked as spies.

The Telegraph

Early forms of communication were dependent on geographical location. That all changed with the invention of the telegraph. The telegraph was a machine that sent electric signals along wires from one place to another and the signals translated into a message. In 1844, Samuel Morse sent the first telegraph message in Morse code, long or short clicks, each combination of sounds representing letters in the alphabet.

Suddenly, humans could send messages over hundreds of kilometres almost instantly. This was the start of telephones and even the Internet!

3 Read the text again and answer the questions.

1 What did a smoke signal represent in many cultures?

----

2 When did carrier pigeons help save many people's lives?

----

3 How did human messengers travel from one place to another?

----

4 What secret job did some human messengers do?

----

4 Find out about your favorite messaging site and tell a partner about it. Think about these questions:

- What type of site is it?
- When did it start?
- Who started it?

- How is it different from communication in the past?
- Why is it your favorite social media platform?

THINK!

How would life be different without a phone or the Internet? How would you communicate?

READING 4

AROUND THE WORLD

THE YORUBA PEOPLE

1 **Look at the images and discuss the questions.**

1 What are these people doing?

2 What types of artwork can you see?

2 🔊 **R.04** **Read and listen to the blog post about the Yoruba people and their art. Were your ideas in Exercise 1 correct?**

Home	Destinations	About	Contact

THE YORUBA: GREAT ARTISTS

The Yoruba are one of the largest ethnic and cultural groups in western Africa and the Yoruba people have lived in urban societies since the 5th century AD. Ile-Ife in Nigeria was the ancient capital city of the Yoruba. Originally, the Yoruba worked as farmers, **traders**, and artists. Nowadays, the Yoruba live in a special cultural region called Yorubaland in the different countries of Nigeria, Benin, and Togo.

The Yoruba have a long tradition in art and many Yoruba people are amazing artists. Their wooden sculptures and terracotta **figures** show animals and people from all levels of society. Yoruba art also includes **pottery**, textiles, and metalwork.

In the Yoruba culture, the head is seen as the center of **power** and many ancient head sculptures made of bronze and teracotta still survive today. The heads are naturalistic in style and have a serene expression. These sculptures may represent kings and queens.

Most Yoruba art has a meaning or purpose. Some items are connected to their **beliefs**, while others are for celebrations. The Yoruba wear different traditional masks and costumes during festivals and ceremonies that can last for days. These masks and costumes are an important part of Yoruba culture. In the Egungun ceremony, the Yoruba make special Egungun masks and costumes, and perform traditional dances to honor their ancestors.

Egungun masks, costumes, and dancing

Traditionally, women and men in Yoruba culture are involved in different artistic trades. The women often make the pots used for cooking and eating, and more unique pots for special occasions, such as ritual bowls. The men are responsible for leather and beadwork. They use animal skins to make things like bags and sandals, and they decorate clothes and crowns for important people with bead designs of human faces, birds, and flowers.

Yoruba art and artists have influenced many artists around the world, and you can see many examples of ancient Yoruba art in many museums.

3 **Read the text again and answer the questions.**

1 Which part of Africa do Yoruba people come from?

 They come from western Africa.

2 What is Yorubaland and where is it?

 ----

3 What are typical materials used in Yoruba art?

 ----

4 Why do the Yoruba make art?

 ----

5 What is typical in many festivals and ceremonies?

 ----

6 Who does artwork in Yoruba culture?

 ----

4 **Complete the sentences with the words in bold in the article.**

1 It's important to respect their _____beliefs_____ although we might not share them.

2 Her parents were market _____, selling fruit and vegetables.

3 His hobby is _____. He makes a lot of beautiful bowls and plates.

4 There were two _____ in the painting, a man and a woman.

5 Amazing artwork has the _____ to inspire people.

 THINK!

Do you think it's important for everyday objects to be beautiful? Why / Why not?

PUZZLES & GAMES

UNIT 1

1 Circle the words for life stages. Then match them with the images.

a poen(take)mhu(a)ok(course)va .....2.....

b fyrgetupawbjobepk ....

c negetwonmarriedjur ....

d bremhaveswachildrenyres ....

e yoctakenikanerdexamlops ....

f hdfeweleaveashomewbgye ....

2 Read the sentences about the future and write the life stages from Exercise 1 the person is talking about.

1 I'd love to work as a designer.
.....get a job.....

2 I'm going to live with three other friends.
....

3 I hope I get a good grade.
....

4 We're going to celebrate with our families.
....

5 Ideally, I'll have three.
....

6 I want to study English this summer.
....

UNIT 2

3 Circle the verbs and then complete the phrases with them.

E	E	Q	I	Y	B	K	L
K	N	K	A	A	U	G	O
A	J	L	A	W	I	E	S
T	P	W	A	M	L	E	D
W	R	T	Y	A	D	K	O
O	C	E	K	A	B	A	U
H	R	W	B	P	G	T	U

1 .... cookies
2 .... board games
3 .... gymnastics
4 .... the sunset
5 .... skateboarding

4 Use the code and write advice. Then match one piece of advice to the image below.

1	2	3	4	5	6	7	8	9	10	11	12	13	14	15	16	17	18	19	20	21	22
E	C	D	A	I	G	U	T	S	F	K	O	P	R	M	L	H	Y	N	W	X	J

a 18 12 7   9 17 12 7 16 3   6 12   8 12
Y o u ....
9 16 1 1 13   1 4 14 16 5 1 14.
....

b 8 17 1 18   9 17 12 7 16 3   8 4 11 1
....
4   20 4 16 11   12 14   3 12
....
1 21 1 14 2 5 9 1.
....

c 17 1   9 17 12 7 16 3   3 12   18 12 6 4.
....

d 9 17 1   9 17 12 7 16 3 19' 8   1 4 8
....
22 7 19 11   10 12 12 3.
....

e 9 17 1   9 17 12 7 16 3 19' 8   9 11 5 13
....
23 14 1 4 11 10 4 9 8   23 1 10 12 14 1
....
9 2 17 12 12 16.
....

f 17 1   9 17 12 7 16 3   22 12 5 19   4
....
6 18 15.
....

The image matches sentence ....

UNIT 3

1 Complete the spiral crossword with the correct advertising words.

1 I saw a great a<u>dvertisement</u> for sneakers yesterday.

2 Some ads p_____ to make you more beautiful, but that's not true!

3 This app is a better v_____ than that one. It has a lot more games.

4 I don't think ads i_____ me. I choose what I like!

5 My favorite l_____ is the one with a bird in the middle.

6 The p_____ was so good, they sold everything in half an hour!

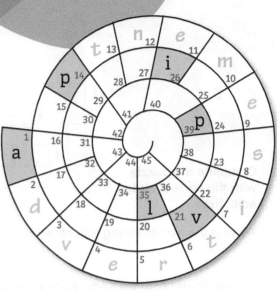

2 Put the words with the same color in the correct order and add *a, to, the* to make correct sentences if necessary. Then match 1–5 with a–e.

watch	have	don't	logo	You
go	passengers	design	it	All
He	have	have	doesn't	have
must	technology	new	grocery store	She
You	has	study	now	ticket

1 ~~You / have / watch / it / now: You have to watch it now.~~ ....b....

2 _____

3 _____

4 _____

5 _____

a You can get what you want at the street market.

b The camerawork is amazing.

c The company wants something completely different.

d Please buy one before you get on the train.

e You don't need to take that course to be a vet.

UNIT 4

3 Find the missing words. Use the extra letters to write the secret question.

1 We ~~R~~D~~E~~O C Y Y O C U L E
   re_____ most of the trash in our house.

2 We P R R O E T E U C S T T E H E
   _____ some of the plastic and cardboard for activities at home.

3 We try to E R N V E I R D O U N M E C E N T
   _____ the number of things we buy by fixing things.

What's the secret question? (26 letters, 5 words)

_____

Answer the question.

_____

4 Complete the zero conditional sentences with the correct verbs.

1 If your house h<u>a s</u> solar panels, it p(_)_____ energy.

2 If your house m___ (_)___ energy, we r___ emissions.

3 If we r___(_)___ emissions, we don't p___ the air so much.

4 If we r___ the amount of CO_2 in the atmosphere, it i(_)better for the environment.

5 We can s___ our planet if we t___(_)action now!

The letters in the circles make an important word. What is it?

_____

UNIT **5**

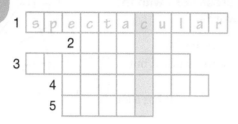

	1	s	p	e	c	t	a	c	u	l	a	r
2												
3												
4												
5												

1 Complete the puzzle with the correct strong adjectives.

What is the secret strong adjective?

----

1 We watched a _____spectacular_____ sunset last night.

2 That's _____. I thought I left my keys on the table, but they aren't there.

3 She was a _____ musician.

4 After skiing all morning, my hands were _____.

5 The jokes were a little _____, but they made me laugh.

2 Put the words with the same color in order to make second conditional questions. Then answer the questions.

1 If _____
_____?

2 _____
_____?

3 _____
_____?

4 _____
_____?

play talent #unoname # what you you were what what choose you if what if what would musician you be uoname one changed you with thing you would op if a a you you had changed if you you name name Earth would instrument special famous

UNIT **6**

3 Follow the maze. Circle the letters to make four types of music and write the words.

a	e	p	l	o	y	e	i	t
(h)	s	j	h	y	m	y	d	v
r	i	b	(r)	p	a	s	v	x
g	e	d	k	g	e	(c)	l	a
p	g	t	(h)	k	e	k	o	p
u	q	a	v	c	g	n	l	u
e	(r)	f	o	r	m	t	o	i
(j)	z	j	o	n	n	u	w	t
e	a	n	z	y	m	j	s	c

1 _____hip-hop_____

2 _____

3 _____

4 _____

5 _____

6 _____

4 Read sentences 1–9 and complete the chart. Then answer the question.

Band	Cuban Band	British Boy Band	Canadian All-Girl Orchestra	South Korean Band
Location of Biggest Concert	_____ _____	Sydney	_____	_____
Type of Music	_____	_____	_____	_____
Size of Band	_____	_____	_____	_____

1 The British band has played in Sydney. It was their biggest concert.

2 The Canadian orchestra has performed in Barcelona. Their concert was a great success and they had their largest audience.

3 The girls have played different types of music, but their usual genre is classical.

4 The seven South Korean bandmates are a famous pop group.

5 The group that usually plays classical music has 32 members.

6 The musicians who have played in Sydney usually play techno music.

7 The South Koreans have played in Rio de Janeiro. Their performance on Copacabana beach attracted a record audience.

8 The number of members in the boy band is one eighth the size of the orchestra.

9 There are five members in the band that plays R & B. They have performed in the US capital.

Which band have played in Washington?

_____

A	C	D	E	G	H	I	L	N	O	P	R	S	T	U	V	Z
§	□	@	∞	*	Ψ	◊	⊢	↙	↕	Δ	Ɔ	Φ	»	¤	㇄	●

1 Use the code to write verbs for achievements.
Then write the noun of the verbs.

1 § □ Ψ ◊ ∞ ㇄ ∞
_a c h i e v e_   _achievement_

2 Φ ¤ Ɔ ㇄ ◊ ㇄ ∞
_____   _____

3 Δ Ɔ ↕ @ ¤ □ ∞
_____   _____

4 @ ∞ ㇄ ∞ ⊢ ↕ Δ
_____   _____

5 ↕ Ɔ * § ↙ ◊ ● ∞
_____   _____

6 @ ◊ Φ □ ↕ ㇄ ∞ Ɔ
_____   _____

2 Start in the center of the spiral. Circle words to make four questions. Answer them with *for* and *since*.

1 Q: ___How long_____
A1: _____
A2: _____

2 Q: _____
A1: _____
A2: _____

3 Q: _____
A1: _____
A2: _____

4 Q: _____
A1: _____
A2: _____

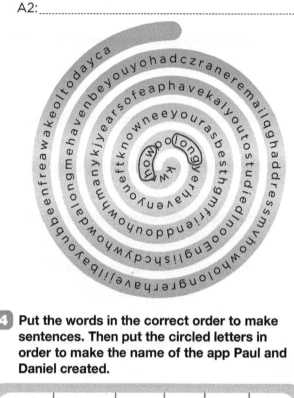

UNIT **8**

3 Put the letters in the correct order to write phrases with *do*, *have*, and *make*.

1 Where can you _d o_ _v o l u n t e e r_ _w o r k_ (ewrdnootvlkouer) where you live?

2 Would you tell someone if you _____ _____ (dherbltuao) with bullies at school?

3 I need to _____ _____ _____ (taydhpsieslaioiiccvt). They make me feel better!

4 If you could do anything in the world, what would you do to _____ _____ (erfaminkdafeeec)?

5 It's difficult for teenagers to _____ _____ (saeocmeksdiin) when there are so many different social influences.

6 Tim _____ _____ (yarphtoudopnatni) to participate in the triathlon race and he _____ _____ (wdlidel). He won third prize!

7 Alison doesn't _____ _____ (eetamhiv) to see her friends after school during the week. She has too much homework.

4 Put the words in the correct order to make sentences. Then put the circled letters in order to make the name of the app Paul and Daniel created.

Paul	They	helped	to	they	lot
were	opportunity	app	years	had	Daniel
(i)nteresting	The(y)	have	(s)ome	alrea(d)y	have
familie(s)	th(i)rteen	an	when	th(e)m	(o)ld
people	(c)reated	a	meet	an	and

1 _Paul and Daniel created an app when they were thirteen years old_

2 _____

3 _____

Name of app: _____ !
What type of app do you think it is?

_____

PROJECT
WRITING A PERSUASIVE TEXT

CREATE AN INFOGRAPHIC ABOUT YOUR SCHOOL'S CARBON FOOTPRINT.

1 Look at the infographic on page 107. What's the infographic about? Check (✓) the correct answer.

1 ○ what people should do to reduce their school's carbon footprint
2 ○ what people should do to calculate their school's carbon footprint

2 Look at the design of the infographic. What do you notice about it? Discuss your ideas with a partner.

3 Look at the writing techniques below. Check (✓) the techniques which are features of a persuasive text. Then find and circle examples of these techniques in the infographic.

1 ✓ repeat key words   5 ○ create suspense
2 ○ explain a process   6 ○ use emotive words
3 ○ use powerful verbs   7 ○ use rhetorical questions
4 ○ include strong adjectives

4 Read the infographic and answer the questions.

1 How much of UK carbon emissions are schools responsible for?

.... *2%* ....

2 What takes about half of a school's energy consumption and what takes about a quarter?

....

3 What should people do if they're not using equipment?

....

4 How can people reduce pollution outside the school?

....

5 Why is it important to use eco-friendly companies to supply products and services for schools?

....

 **PROJECT TASK**

 THINK!

Is reducing your carbon footprint a priority in your community? Why / Why not?

1 PLAN

1 Find out about your school's carbon footprint. Search for and use an online "school carbon footprint calculator."
2 Think about the design of your infographic. Look for images and information to use.
3 Write a first version of your text. Remember to include information about your school, the main areas that have an impact on the school's carbon footprint, and suggestions of ways to reduce it.
4 Finalize your text. Remember to include the features of a persuasive text from Exercise 2.
5 Design and create a final version of your infographic with the text and images.
6 Check grammar, spelling, and punctuation, and practice pronunciation of any difficult words.

2 YOUR DIGITAL PORTFOLIO

Upload your infographic to the class portfolio for everyone to see! Present your infographic to the class.

3 REFLECT

Which features of a persuasive text did you include in your infographic? How do they make your text more persuasive?

Time Is Running Out
Catastrophic climate change is here!

Do we want to make a BIG difference in our future?

Do something now!

Reduce our school's carbon footprint!

Catastrophic climate change is one of the most serious problems in the 21st century. And it is human activities that generate the carbon emissions that cause climate change. Take schools, for example. Schools in the UK are responsible for **2%** of the country's TOTAL carbon emissions. How?

School energy use The amount of energy a school uses is huge. Did you know that **37%** of a school's carbon footprint comes from energy use? School buildings use a lot of electricity. Heating is about **50%** of total energy consumption in schools in the UK and lighting is about **20–25%**. So it makes sense to reduce unnecessary waste. Close doors while the heat is on and switch off equipment when we're not using it.

Reduce energy waste in the school buildings!

Travel How can we reduce pollution outside the school? More teachers, parents, and students should walk or cycle to and from school! Let's build better walking and cycling paths to help people to walk to school.

Reduce pollution from travel to and from school!

Companies that supply products and services

At our school, there are paper towels or hand dryers in restrooms, sports equipment, furniture, laptops, and electrical equipment which all come from different companies. If we make sure that each company is eco-friendly, then we know that it doesn't create as many emissions as a non-eco-friendly company and that it takes good care of the environment. For example, it uses less plastic, or uses solar energy to produce its products. And, we need to take care of the things in our school so they last longer!

Reduce emissions by using eco-friendly companies to supply products and services!

REDUCE WASTE at our school and stop contributing to global climate change! Act now and make a BIG difference in our future!

PROJECT
DESIGNING A BOARD GAME OR CARD GAME

1 Look at the title and contents of the board game on page 109 and answer the questions.

1 Who's the game for?

....

2 What do you need to play this game?

....

2 Read the introduction to the description of the game and complete the chart.

Name of Game	
Aim of Game	
How to Win	

3 Read the whole description and answer the questions.

1 How many players can play the game? .... 2–4 ....
2 Where do players put their counters to start the game? ....
3 Who starts the game? ....
4 If a player falls on a Dilemma square who takes a Dilemma card? ....
5 What happens if the player suggests the correct solution to the dilemma? ....
6 What happens on an Oops! square? ....

PROJECT TASK

1 PLAN

1 Choose a type of game to design: a board game or a card game, and decide who the game is for.

2 Decide what you need in order to play the game, the aim of the game, how to win, how to play the game, and what the game will look like. Look for images or draw your own.

3 Write a first version of the description of your game. Remember to include the name, an introduction to your game explaining who the game is for, the aim of the game and how to win, the contents, and clear instructions on how to play the game.

4 Design and create a final version of the description of your game, and include images to make the game look attractive.

5 Check grammar, spelling, punctuation, and practice pronunciation of any difficult words.

THINK!

Why do think people play board or card games? What can you learn from playing these games?

2 YOUR DIGITAL PORTFOLIO

Upload your game to the class portfolio for everyone to see! Present your game to the class.

3 REFLECT

Which is your favorite game? Why?

DILEMMA TEENS

Contents
- board
- 24 **Dilemma** cards
- 4 counters
- dice

Dilemma Teens is the teen version of the exciting, fast-moving Dilemma board game. Solve the teen dilemmas and be the first player to reach Home Sweet Home to win the game.

How to Play (2–4 players)

- Each player places his/her counter on the **Big Wide World** square.
- The oldest player (Player A) starts by throwing the dice and moving the counter the number of squares shown on the dice.
- If Player A falls on a **Dilemma** square, Player B (or one of the other players) takes the top card from the **Dilemma** cards and reads the dilemma aloud. Player A suggests a solution to the dilemma. Player B looks at the bottom of the card and reads out the answer. If Player A's answer is correct, he/she moves to the next square. If the answer is incorrect, he/she stays on the square.

- Play continues with Player B's turn to throw the dice and move the counter (and then Player C, etc. if there are more than 2 players).
- If a player lands on an **Oops!** square, then he/she has to follow the instructions on the square, for example:
  Go to the principal's office = Lose a turn
  You miss the bus and arrive late = Go back 3 squares
- Play continues until a player reaches the **Home Sweet Home** square and wins the game!

IRREGULAR VERBS

Infinitive	Simple Past	Past Participle
be	was / were	been
beat	beat	beaten
become	became	become
begin	began	begun
break	broke	broken
bring	brought	brought
build	built	built
buy	bought	bought
catch	caught	caught
choose	chose	chosen
come	came	come
cost	cost	cost
cut	cut	cut
do	did	done
draw	drew	drawn
drink	drank	drunk
drive	drove	driven
eat	ate	eaten
fall	fell	fallen
feel	felt	felt
fight	fought	fought
find	found	found
fly	flew	flown

Infinitive	Simple Past	Past Participle
forget	forgot	forgotten
get	got	got / gotten
give	gave	given
go	went	gone
grow	grew	grown
have	had	had
hear	heard	heard
hide	hid	hidden
hit	hit	hit
hold	held	held
keep	kept	kept
know	knew	known
leave	left	left
lose	lost	lost
make	made	made
meet	met	met
pay	paid	paid
put	put	put
read	read	read
ride	rode	ridden
ring	rang	rung
run	ran	run
say	said	said

Infinitive	Simple Past	Past Participle
see	saw	seen
sell	sold	sold
send	sent	sent
show	showed	shown
shut	shut	shut
sing	sang	sung
sit	sat	sat
sleep	slept	slept
speak	spoke	spoken
spend	spent	spent
stand	stood	stood
swim	swam	swum
take	took	taken
teach	taught	taught
tell	told	told
think	thought	thought
throw	threw	thrown
understand	understood	understood
wake	woke	woken
wear	wore	worn
win	won	won
write	wrote	written

WORKBOOK CONTENTS

1 MY LIFE PLAN

 LANGUAGE REFERENCE

Will and *Be going to*

	Will for Predictions	*Be going to* for Intentions
Affirmative (+)	I think I**'ll live** abroad when I'm older. Perhaps she**'ll be** an engineer.	I**'m going to learn** to drive. They**'re going to get** married.
Negative (–)	He **won't get** the grades he needs. She probably **won't go** to university.	I**'m not going to study** French. We**'re not going to take** the same course.
Questions (?)	**Will** Rosa **take** the exam? **Will** they **go** to the same college?	**Are** you **going to leave** home? **Is** he **going to work** in Hong Kong? When **are** we **going to visit** them?

We often use *will* with *I believe, I (don't) think, I'm sure, maybe, perhaps, probably*.

Reflexive Pronouns

Singular	Plural
I often **talk to myself** when I'm working. You **enjoyed yourself** last time you played tennis. She **introduced herself** to us. He **cut himself** with a knife while he was cooking. My phone **turns itself** off when it's too hot.	We **test ourselves** at the end of each class. OK everyone, **give yourselves** ten minutes to rest before the next game. Art is a natural way for children to **express themselves**.

By + myself, yourself, etc. means *alone, on one's own*.

Life Stages

finish school

get a job

get married

go to college

graduate

have children

leave home

retire

take a course

take an exam

Studying

get a good grade

make progress

practice

prepare

review

take a break

VOCABULARY

1 **Label the images with the words/phrases below.**

- ~~get a job~~ • get married • graduate • have children • leave home • take an exam

get a job

2 **Match 1–6 with a–f.**

1 My sister says she's not going to have ___*b*___
2 He's very interested in languages and he wants to take ___
3 A month after Amy left college, she got ___
4 At 65 my grandad decided to ___
5 In my country, most children finish ___
6 After school, my older brother went ___

a a really good job.
b children.
c school at 18.
d retire.
e a course in Italian.
f to college to study music.

3 **Put the letters in the correct order and complete the sentences.**

1 Did Carlo get a good _____*grade*_____ (ragde) in his French test?
2 My reading and writing is OK, but I need to _____ (capritec) my speaking skills more.
3 My English course is going really well. I'm definitely making _____ (rogperss).
4 We have to _____ (evrewi) some vocabulary for our class on Friday.
5 Remember to take a _____ (ekarb) every hour or so when you're studying.
6 Unfortunately, Evie didn't have enough time to _____ (erparpe) for her exam.

4 **Complete the dialogue with the correct words/phrases for studying.**

Mariana   Your mom says you're studying Spanish, Isabel. How's it going?

Isabel   OK, I think. My teacher says I'm making good ¹____*progress*____. I'm certainly better than I was last year!

Mariana   That's great to hear!

Isabel   But I find listening difficult. I need to ²_____ that more.

Mariana   Mmm ... I think listening is the hardest part of learning a language.

Isabel   Anyway, I'd better go. I'm ³_____ for a vocabulary test tomorrow and I really want to get ⁴_____. I have a lot of words to ⁵_____.

Mariana   Well good luck and go for a walk or something after an hour or two. Don't forget to ⁶_____!

GRAMMAR

1 Put the words in the correct order.

1 with / will / probably / disagree / us / he .
    He will probably disagree with us.

2 going / to / I'm / try to / job in / get a / a café .
    _____

3 next / grandma / your / retire / will / year ?
    _____

4 will / the / enjoy / sure / I'm / movie / you .
    _____

5 get / Margarita / are / and Carlos / to / married / going ?
    _____

6 angry / think / I / parents / don't / will be / your / with you .
    _____

7 a / not / have / going / we're / to / sleepover .
    _____

8 won't / it / rainy / afternoon / be / this .
    _____

2 Cross out the six incorrect words and write the correct words below.

Hey Alicia, how are you doing? Are you feeling better now? Raquel and I are going to ~~having~~ a picnic in the park tomorrow. Can you come? We're meeting at 4 by the lake – it won't being so crowded then. I'm going to bringing food and Raquel are going to bring drinks. It will being hot so remember your hat! I going to invite Julia, too. Hope to see you tomorrow.

6:25

1 _____ have _____
2 _____
3 _____
4 _____
5 _____
6 _____

3 Match 1–6 with a–f.

1 Painting and drawing helps me to express ___*e*___
2 By the age of 13, he could take care of _____
3 To practice your pronunciation, you can record _____
4 My eight-year-old sister made this beautiful cake by _____
5 The party was great. We really enjoyed _____
6 By 2030, all new cars will be able to drive _____

a yourself.
b themselves.
c herself.
d himself.
e myself.
f ourselves.

4 Complete the sentences with the correct simple past form of the verbs below and the correct reflexive pronoun.

• build   • cut   • ~~give~~   • look at   • make   • teach

After studying for three hours, he _____ *gave himself* _____ a break.

Abigail and Emma _____ _____ some breakfast.

He _____ in the mirror.

Joe accidentally _____
_____ .

Marcela _____
to play the guitar.

They _____ a new kitchen.

READING

1 **Read the text quickly and check (✓) the correct answers.**

1 Why does Laura email her grandfather?
- ○ to ask him for a job
- ○ to tell him what she's going to do next year
- ○ to ask if she can stay with him

2 What are Laura's plans?
- ○ to work
- ○ to travel
- ○ to work and then travel

To: Felipe Oliveira

Hi Grandpa

Thanks for your message on Sunday. I took my last exam yesterday (geography) so I was studying all week. I *think* my exams went OK. 😶 Computer science was fun (!), but math was difficult. I really hope I get good grades. I guess we'll see in August … 👆

Anyway, you asked about my plans, so here they are! I'm going to take a break from studying before I go to college. I'd like to go traveling for a few months next year, but it will be expensive so I'm going to get a job here and earn some money first. I'm sure you remember my best friend Helena. She and another classmate, Ryan, work in a café on the weekends (see the photo) and I'm going to work there for 15 hours a week starting in July. It's not far from our house so I'll cycle there and back. I'll probably try to get some other work too, maybe at the mall in town. I hope I'll have enough money to go traveling next March.

And where will I go on my trip? Well, probably Italy so I can practice my Italian. Aunt Sofia and Uncle Luca said I can stay with them, which is exciting. I'd love to see my cousins again and I'd like to see Rome again too – Aunt Sofia took this amazing photo of the Colosseum the other evening! Can you believe I was only eight years old the last time we visited them?

Anyway, I'll finish this email now and go and make myself some breakfast. I hope you're well.
Speak soon!
Love,
Laura

2 **Read the text and write *T* (true) or *F* (false) next to the statements.**

1 Laura's grandfather emailed her last weekend. ___T___
2 Laura's computer science exam was easier than her math exam. _____
3 She's going to work in her best friend's café. _____
4 She will take the bus to and from the café. _____
5 She hopes to get two jobs. _____
6 Laura's relations in Italy invited her to stay with them. _____

3 **Write answers to the questions.**

1 Which exam did Laura enjoy?
_____ She enjoyed the computer science exam. _____

2 When will Laura know the results of her exams?
_____

3 What did Laura's grandfather ask her about in his last email?
_____

4 Where will Laura look for a second job?
_____

5 What three reasons does Laura give for going to Italy?
_____

2
WHAT MAKES US HAPPY?

 LANGUAGE REFERENCE

Should/Shouldn't for Advice

Affirmative (+)	Negative (–)	Questions (?)
You **should take** a break.	You **shouldn't eat** so much sugar.	**Should** I **call** him?
He **should eat** more fruit and vegetables.	She **shouldn't sit** down all day.	**Should** he **go** for a run?
I think they **should do** more exercise.	They **shouldn't drink** all that cola.	**Should** we **leave** now?

Tag Questions

Affirmative (+) Sentence	Negative (–) Tag
I'm early,	aren't I?
You eat fish,	don't you?
He told you,	didn't he?
She's Spanish,	isn't she?
It was crowded,	wasn't it?
We can leave now,	can't we?
They're having a sleepover,	aren't they?

Negative (–) Sentence	Affirmative (+) Tag
I was anxious,	wasn't I?
You weren't late,	were you?
Paolo isn't angry,	is he?
She isn't doing yoga,	is she?
She didn't retire,	did she?
You can't buy tickets now,	can you?
They don't play in a band,	do they?

The negative tag for *I am* (*I'm*) is *aren't I?*.

More Free-time Activities

bake cookies   make jewelry

build models   play board games

do gymnastics   take a walk

do yoga   take singing lessons

go skateboarding   watch the sunset

Health and Fitness

go for a run   reduce stress

make friends   stay in shape

prevent diseases   work out

VOCABULARY

1 Complete the sentences with the correct form of the verbs below. Then match images a–f with sentences 1–6.

- build   - ~~do~~   - do   - go   - play   - watch

1 Do you ....*do*............ yoga at school? ....*f*....
2 We .... skateboarding last weekend. ....
3 Shall we climb the hill and .... the sunset? ....
4 They .... gymnastics when they were younger. ....
5 Two of the students were .... a model. ....
6 I love .... board games with my family. ....

| a | b | c |
| d | e | f |

2 Match 1–6 with a–f.

1 My sister makes ....*c*....
2 How often does Martina go ....
3 Serena and I baked ....
4 Do you still take ....
5 Would you like to play ....
6 Danny and I took ....

a a walk by the river.
b a board game?
c her own jewelry.
d singing lessons?
e skateboarding?
f some cookies yesterday.

3 Put the letters in the correct order and complete the sentences.

1 I work ....*out*............ (uto) at the gym three times a week.
2 He stays in .... (haspe) by swimming and running.
3 My mom goes for a .... (urn) before work in the mornings.
4 Yoga is really good for .... (icegrudn) stress.
5 Regular exercise can help .... (rtenpev) some diseases.
6 Joining a soccer team helped Camila to .... (aekm) friends.

4 Complete the text with correct form of the verbs in Exercise 3.

There are so many benefits to exercise. It can [1] ....*reduce*............ stress, it helps you to [2] .... in shape and doctors say it can even [3] .... diseases. There are so many different exercise options, too, and some of them are free. For example, you can take a walk or [4] .... for a run without spending any money, or you can [5] .... out in your own living room. Joining a running club or a gym can also help you to [6] .... friends. So choose your exercise and get started!

COMMENT   SHARE   LIKE

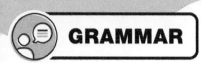

GRAMMAR

1 Complete the sentences with *should* or *shouldn't* and the verbs below.

- drink   • eat   • practice   • spend   • use   • ~~walk~~

1 My dad _____ should walk _____ more and drive less.
2 You _____ your English every day.
3 Theo _____ his phone so much.
4 People _____ so much junk food.
5 We _____ so much time at our computers.
6 Marta _____ more water.

2 Read about Daniel. Then use the phrases to write sentences with *should* or *shouldn't* giving him advice.

> Daniel is often tired in class and can't concentrate on his work. He wants to be healthier and more active, but he always plays video games in the evening and goes to bed late. In the mornings, he finds it difficult to get up, and he doesn't have time for breakfast. He lives quite near his school, but because he's always late, he takes the bus.

1 go to bed earlier
_____ He should go to bed earlier. _____

2 play video games late in the evening
_____

3 get up an hour before school starts
_____

4 eat a healthy breakfast before he goes to school
_____

5 take the bus to school
_____

6 walk to school
_____

3 Circle the correct options.

1 You didn't see Eduardo, *do /(did)*you?
2 They got married, *weren't / didn't* they?
3 It was exciting, *wasn't / was* it?
4 They're staying with their cousins, *don't / aren't* they?
5 Brenda can speak Italian, *can't / doesn't* she?
6 The restaurant isn't expensive, *isn't / is* it?

4 Complete the dialogue with the correct tag questions.

A You weren't at Enzo's party, [1] ____ were you? ____
B Yes, I was!
A Of course you were, sorry! You didn't see Samuel there, [2] _____
B No, I didn't.
A We're meeting Samuel at two o'clock, [3] _____
B Yes, in the café.
A But we're not eating there [4] _____
B No, that's right.
A You eat fish, [5] _____
B Yes, I love fish.
A But you don't eat meat, [6] _____
B No, that's right.

 **READING**

1 **Read the text quickly and check (✓) the correct answers.**

1 Why is Ana worried?
  ○ her friend isn't getting good grades at school
  ○ her friend is working too hard

2 What's Ana going to do?
  ○ visit her friend and do some activities together
  ○ help her friend with her work

MARCIA

Hey, Marcia, you weren't at Paolo's party, were you? 😕 Are you OK?
11:20 pm

Hey, Ana! Good to hear from you. Yeah, I'm fine, thanks. I was just busy that evening. Did you have fun?
11:20 pm

Yeah, it was a really good party, but Patricia and I were sad you weren't there. 😔 You usually like going to parties, don't you?
11:20 pm

Yes, I do, but I was studying that evening. I had a French test on Monday so I was reviewing some vocabulary. To be honest, I didn't really want to go. I wasn't feeling very sociable – I was anxious about the test. And next week I have another test …
11:22 pm

But you always get good grades. Do you remember the last French test? You got over 90%, didn't you? I think you study too hard. I hope you're remembering to take a break – do some yoga or take a walk or something.
11:23 pm

No, I'm too busy.
11:23 pm

Marcia, I'm serious now – I'm worried about you! It's not healthy to study all the time, is it? Even our teachers tell us we shouldn't work all the time! I really think you should give yourself a break. Listen, I've got a plan! I'm going to come round this weekend and we're going to bake some of those amazing chocolate cookies and play some board games. How does that sound?
11:24 pm

That sounds great. It'll be really nice to see you, Ana. You're a good friend! ❤️
11:25 pm

---

2 **Read the text and circle the correct options.**

1 Ana wants to know why Marcia wasn't at *school /* *a party.*

2 Marcia was *ill / studying* last Saturday evening.

3 Ana *enjoyed / didn't enjoy* Paolo's party.

4 Ana thinks Marcia should study *more / less.*

5 Ana wants to visit Marcia and *play board games / do yoga* together.

6 Marcia says she *is too busy / would like* to see Ana.

3 **Write answers to the questions.**

1 Who missed Marcia at Paolo's party as well as Ana?
  Patricia missed Marcia at Paolo's party as well as Ana.

2 What did Marcia do on Monday?

3 How was Marcia feeling on Saturday night?

4 What grade did Marcia get in her last French test?

5 What two things are Marcia and Ana going to do on the weekend?

3 CONSUMER WORLD

 LANGUAGE REFERENCE

Have to and Must

Have to		
Affirmative: Obligation		
I/You/We/They	**have to**	get a visa.
He/She	**has to**	
Negative: No Obligation		
I/You/We/They	**don't have to**	take the bus.
He/She	**doesn't have to**	

Must		
Affirmative: Obligation		
I/You/We/They/He/She	**must**	tell the teacher.
Negative: Prohibition		
I/You/We/They/He/She	**must not**	be late.

We use *must not* to say something is the wrong thing to do.

Have to: Questions and Short Answers

Do I **have to wear** my uniform? **Do** you **have to pay** for medicine? **Do** we **have to take** our shoes off? **Do** they **have to show** their passports?	Yes, I/you/we/they **do**. / No, I/you/we/they **don't**.
Does he **have to go** to the principal's office? **Does** she **have to sign** this?	Yes, he/she **does**. / No, he/she **doesn't**.
How many exams **does** he **have to take**? Why **do** they **have to leave** tomorrow?	

We use *There <u>was</u>* for singular nouns and *There <u>were</u>* for plural nouns.

Advertising

advertise
advertisement
attract
headline
influence

logo
persuade
product
promise
value

Money

cost
invest
label

on sale
own
sell

VOCABULARY

1 Circle eight more advertising words.

proadvertisefomlogomumpersuadezoheadlinepretinfluencewsproductklasvaluebreypromiserattract

1 ____advertise____   4 _____   7 _____

2 _____   5 _____   8 _____

3 _____   6 _____   9 _____

2 Match 1–6 with a–f.

1 advertisement ___e___   3 headline _____   5 product _____

2 attract _____   4 logo _____   6 promise _____

a line of words in large letters at the top of an advertisement or a story in a newspaper, etc.

b image or symbol that a company uses to sell things

c tell someone that you will certainly do something

d thing that a company makes and sells

e picture, short film, etc. that tries to make people buy something

f make people interested in something

3 Put the letters in the correct order and complete the sentences.

1 I usually wait till clothes are _____on sale_____ (no esal) before I buy them.

2 The government needs to _____ (venits) more money in transportation.

3 Excuse me, how much does this jacket _____ (soct)?

4 We went to a store that sells clothes by her favorite _____ (balle).

5 I never wear those blue sneakers. I think I'll _____ (lesl) them.

6 How many hats do you _____ (won), Leticia?

4 Complete the dialogue with the correct form of the words/phrases below.

• cost   • invest   • label   • on sale   • own   • sell

Sophie   Hey, look at these jeans! I really love this ¹ _____label_____. They make the best jeans.

Aline   Yeah, they're really cool. Are you going to buy them?

Sophie   I can't afford them. They ² _____ far too much!

Aline   No, they're ³ _____. Look – they're half price!

Sophie   Wow, that's a bargain! I can't buy them though. I already ⁴ _____ five pairs of jeans and my mom thinks that's four too many. She doesn't understand why I like nice clothes. She never spends money on things like that. She just ⁵ _____ her money so she can earn more money.

Aline   You have five pairs of jeans, did you say?

Sophie   Yeah, although I don't wear all of them.

Aline   Well, maybe you could ⁶ _____ the jeans that you don't wear, and then you can buy these?

Sophie   That's a good idea, Aline – thanks!

GRAMMAR

1 Complete the dialogue with the words below.

- don't   • has   • have (x 2)   • must   • ~~to~~

Bruna   Do you have any rules in your house?

Joseph   Yes, one or two. We have ¹_____to_____ do some work around the house to get our pocket money. So, my brother ²_____ to clean the bathroom once a week and I ³_____ to wash my mom's car. What about you?

Bruna   Well, one important rule is that we ⁴_____ to eat in the kitchen. We ⁵_____ not eat in our bedrooms or in the living room.

Joseph   That's the same in my house.

Bruna   But we're lucky. We ⁶_____ have to do any jobs to get our pocket money.

Joseph   You are lucky!

2 Circle the correct options.

1 Remember, you (must not) / don't have to be late for your exam!
2 You must not / don't have to bring any food to the picnic. We're taking enough for all of us.
3 We must get to Gabriel's house by six o'clock so we really must not / don't have to miss the bus.
4 Luke can come to the party with me if he likes but he must not / doesn't have to.
5 Beatriz will need her passport with her so tell her she must not / doesn't have to forget it.
6 You must not / don't have to pay for the concert – it's free!

3 Complete the mini dialogues with the correct form of *do* or *have*.

1 **A** _____Do_____ you sometimes _____have_____ to cook for your family?
   B No, I _____don't_____.
2 **A** _____ they _____ to pay for their school books?
   B Yes, they _____.
3 **A** _____ she _____ to save any of her pocket money?
   B No, she _____.
4 **A** _____ he _____ to get a good grade?
   B Yes, he _____.

4 Write questions and answers with the prompts and *have to*.

1 Claudia / get up / early?
   no / she

   _____Does Claudia have to get up early?_____

   _____No, she doesn't._____

2 you / take / a course?
   yes / I

   _____

   _____

3 Rosa and Miguel / get / a visa?
   no / they

   _____

   _____

4 he / drive / there?
   yes / he

   _____

   _____

5 they / pay for / tickets?
   no / they

   _____

   _____

6 we / speak English?
   yes / we

   _____

   _____

 **READING**

1 **Read the text quickly and check (✓) the correct answers.**

1 How do most young people born between
approximately 1995 and 2005 feel about ads?
- ○ They don't like any of them.
- ○ They don't like digital advertisements.
- ○ They don't like traditional advertisements.

2 What are companies doing about this?
- ○ They're not investing in traditional ads to attract young people.
- ○ They're investing in other ways of attracting young people.

Get the marketing news that matters each day.

GEN Z HATE YOUR ADS!

David Smith on February 10 at 6:32

A recent study of young people's attitudes towards advertisements revealed some interesting facts. Young people born between approximately 1995 and 2005, (often called Generation Z or, informally Gen Z), hate advertisements! However, to be more precise, they don't hate all ads. They hate a specific type of advertisement – the digital or online ad.

In the study, almost 70% of young people born between these dates said they preferred more traditional advertisements, for example on billboards at the side of the street or on buses. As one young person explained: "When I walk or cycle along a street, I can choose to look at the ads, but I don't have to. When I'm using my cell phone and companies are advertising all these products, I have to see them – I have no choice." Companies that make products for young people are listening to them and are now investing more in traditional advertisements.

The study shows that young people have clear ideas about the sort of ads they want to see. Most said that they didn't like advertisements in which the logo was very obvious, and they didn't like to see celebrities advertising products. They are more likely to listen to influencers. They liked advertisements that told interesting stories or were funny or creative. They also liked great music in their ads.

So why is this? Well, perhaps it's because this generation watches movies and series online where there are no advertisements. This is the norm for them. It's clear that in the future, companies will have to find different ways to attract young people to their products.

---

2 **Read the text and complete each sentence with one word.**

1 A recent study investigated young people's __attitudes__ towards ads.

2 _____ Z refers to young people born between approximately 1995 and 2005.

3 Traditional advertisements on _____ at the side of the street or on buses are the type of ads that most young people prefer.

4 _____ are more successful than celebrities in attracting young people to a product.

5 It is the _____ for this group of young people to watch movies and series without ads.

3 **Write answers to the questions.**

1 What percentage of this group of young people prefer more traditional advertisements?
_____Over 70% of this group of young people prefer more traditional advertisements._____

2 Why do these young people prefer traditional advertisements?
_____

3 What don't they like to be obvious in advertisements?
_____

4 What do they like to hear in advertisements?
_____

5 How do young people usually watch movies and series?
_____

4 WE CAN SAVE OUR PLANET

 LANGUAGE REFERENCE

Zero Conditional and First Conditional

Zero Conditional	
If Clause (*If* + Simple Present)	Result Clause (Simple Present)
If you **mix** red and yellow,	you **get** orange.
If you **buy** recycled products,	you **save** energy.

First Conditional	
If Clause (*If* + Simple Present)	Result Clause (*will/won't* + Infinitive)
If the weather **improves**,	we **will go** out.
If we all **drive** less,	the air **will be** cleaner.
If she **fails** her exams,	she **won't go** to college.

The *if* clause can come first or second in zero and first conditional sentences. If the *if* clause comes second, we don't use a comma: *You get orange if you mix red and yellow.*

May and *Might* for Possibility

Affirmative (+)	I **may go** to the mall after class. We **might see** you at the weekend. Leonardo **might be** able to help us.
Negative (–)	They **may not come** to the party. She **might not have** enough money to go on vacation.

We don't usually use *may* and *might* in questions. We can form questions using *Is it possible that …?* or *Do you think …?*.

The Environment

cut down	reduce
destroy	reuse
pollute	throw away
protect	turn off
recycle	waste

Verbs and Phrases + Prepositions

agree with	succeed in
depend on	take care of
pay attention to	worry about

⊜ **VOCABULARY**

1 **Look at the images and complete the sentences with the correct environment words.**

We make sure we never
___throw away___ any food.

You can _____ bottles, paper, and plastic in town.

Remember to _____ the light when you leave a room.

We must not _____ so many trees.

A lot of vehicles _____ the air in all our cities.

Governments aren't doing enough to _____ the planet.

2 **Check (✓) the two words/phrases that complete each sentence.**

1 We must recycle more of our …
  a ⊘ plastic.   b ⊘ glass.   c ◯ rivers.

2 We are polluting our …
  a ◯ air.   b ◯ trash.   c ◯ oceans.

3 We currently waste a lot of …
  a ◯ energy.   b ◯ water.   c ◯ air.

4 Unfortunately, we are destroying …
  a ◯ the air.   b ◯ the planet.   c ◯ the environment.

5 We must try to reduce …
  a ◯ plastic use.   b ◯ CO_2 emissions.   c ◯ water.

6 At the end of the day, make sure you turn off any …
  a ◯ computers.   b ◯ lights.   c ◯ energy.

7 You can reuse …
  a ◯ bags.   b ◯ air.   c ◯ plastic bottles.

3 **Complete the dialogue with the correct words.**

A Do you worry [1]_____about_____ the environment?

B Yes, I do. We should do more to take care [2]_____ our planet. Our future depends [3]_____ it.

A I agree [4]_____ you. If we destroy it, there won't be a future for people. Politicians should pay attention [5]_____ young people like you – I'm sure you'll succeed [6]_____ making them listen.

4 **Match 1–6 with a–f.**

1 I'm not sure I agree ___d___
2 We need to pay attention _____
3 The campaign succeeded _____
4 We really must take more care _____
5 Most young people worry _____
6 We all depend _____

a to what scientists are saying.
b on nature for our existence.
c about climate change.
d with you.
e of our oceans.
f in reducing food waste.

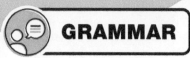

GRAMMAR

1 Complete the zero conditional sentences using the correct form of the verbs below.

• add   • break   • get   • ~~go~~   • turn off   • use

1   If I _____go_____ to bed late, I feel tired the next day.
2   The sauce tastes a lot better if you _____ a little salt to it.
3   If you drop a plate on this floor, it _____.
4   You save electricity if you _____ your computer at night.
5   If public transportation is reliable, people _____ their cars less.
6   I'm always very happy if I _____ good grades in my tests.

2 Complete the first conditional sentences using the verbs in parentheses.

1   Harry _____will make_____ (make) more progress if he _____studies_____ (study) harder.
2   If you _____ (do) more exercise, you _____ (feel) healthier.
3   If it _____ (rain) this afternoon, we _____ (drive) to the bowling alley.
4   I _____ (tell) Luis about the party if I _____ (see) him at lunchtime.
5   If we _____ (take) our bikes on vacation, we _____ (not need) to use the car.
6   If she _____ (stays) here any longer, she _____ (not be) in time for the talk.

3 Complete the sentences using *may* or *might* and the verbs in parentheses.

What are these people's plans for today?

Charlotte _might go for a run_.
(might / go)

Tom _____.
(may / take)

She _____.
(may / bake)

He _____.
(might / do)

They _____.
(may / play)

He _____.
(might / go)

4 Rewrite the sentences using the words in parentheses.

1   It's possible that he will agree with us. (may)
    _____He may agree with us._____

2   Perhaps she's not at home. (might)
    _____

3   Maybe we'll persuade Yolanda to come with us. (might)
    _____

4   There's a chance the sneakers are on sale. (may)
    _____

5   It's possible that we'll be able to stop climate change. (might)
    _____

6   Perhaps he won't have time to finish the model. (may)
    _____

 **READING**

1 Read the text quickly and check (✓) the correct answers.

1 Why does Samuel Carvalho write blog posts?
- ○ to tell readers how to make vegetarian food
- ○ to tell people about environmentally friendly ways to travel
- ○ to persuade readers to do things that protect the planet

2 What does Samuel suggest we should do?
- ○ continue doing activities that may destroy the planet
- ○ stop doing activities that may destroy the planet
- ○ reduce activities that may destroy the planet

● ● ● ●   _ □ X

A Future With No Fun?

ABOUT ME

Posted on July 25th **by Samuel Carvalho**

We all depend on a healthy planet for our future. The problem is, our planet isn't healthy and we really have to do something about it before it's too late. You know the advice – you read it all the time:

- stop traveling by airplane and car
- stop buying new things and start reusing the things that you already own
- stop eating meat

But it's difficult, isn't it? We don't want to stop enjoying ourselves. There are beautiful parts of the world we want to visit, exciting new products we want to own, and interesting dishes we want to try (some with meat). We don't want to stop

doing and having these things, so we pay no attention to the advice.

But there might be another way ... Maybe we don't have to stop completely, just reduce what we do, for example:

- fly once a year
- only buy two pieces of clothing in summer, two in winter, etc.
- eat vegetarian food half of the week

These are small changes that everyone can make and then we won't pollute the atmosphere as much and we'll waste a lot less. Perhaps, if we all make these small changes to our lives, we'll have a future on Earth.

My name is Samuel Carvalho and I want you to change the way you live in order to take care of our planet! (Actually, if you don't eat meat and never fly or buy anything new, don't change a thing! You can still read my posts, though!) ☺

2 Read the text and complete each sentence with one word.

1 Samuel wants his readers to take care of the _____planet_____.

2 The advice we all know tells us to stop buying _____ things.

3 It also tells us to stop eating _____.

4 Samuel says no one wants to stop _____ themselves.

5 He says perhaps we should _____ just once a year.

6 He says perhaps we should eat _____ food half of the week.

3 Write answers to the questions.

1 Which vehicles does Samuel mention?
_____He mentions airplanes and cars._____

2 According to Samuel, what do we all want to visit?
_____

3 What do we all want to own?
_____

4 How many pieces of clothing does Samuel suggest we buy?
_____

5 If we make these small changes, what two good things will happen?
_____

5 MY ONLINE SELF

 LANGUAGE REFERENCE

Second Conditional

If Clause (*If* + Simple Past)	Result Clause (*would/wouldn't* + Infinitive)
If I **had** more time,	I **would learn** another language.
If she **worked** harder,	she **would get** better grades.
If we **took** care of the environment,	we **wouldn't have** all these issues.
Questions (?)	
If you **had** a problem, **would** you tell your teacher? What **would** you **say** if Nicolas **invited** you to go on vacation with him?	

To talk about unreal conditions, we use *would/wouldn't* (not *will/won't*).

Indefinite Pronouns

Affirmative (+)	Negative (–)	Questions (?)
Someone posted a photo of him online.	I didn't see **anyone** I knew in town. **No one** told me he was ill.	Did **anyone** comment on your post?
Could you buy **something** to take to the party tonight?	I didn't see **anything** I wanted to buy.	Is there **anything** we can do to help?
They don't sell ice cream here – let's go **somewhere** else.	I can't find my phone **anywhere**. Young people have **nowhere** to go in the evenings round here.	Did you go **anywhere** nice this summer?

Strong Adjectives

brilliant	silly
crazy	spectacular
freezing	ugly
huge	useless
shocking	weird

The Internet

download	screenshot
file	search
password	tweet
post	upload

VOCABULARY

1 Find eight strong adjectives.

A	M	L	S	I	L	L	Y	C	I	P
V	D	P	I	K	J	R	T	U	F	M
I	S	S	E	F	C	R	U	Z	E	Q
U	H	U	G	E	S	A	G	G	N	U
K	O	E	S	U	S	E	L	E	S	S
L	C	C	D	U	I	L	Y	D	F	T
D	K	T	C	R	A	Z	Y	I	O	U
E	I	G	Y	T	B	E	R	J	A	S
D	N	F	R	E	E	Z	I	N	G	E
U	G	H	E	M	V	S	S	E	R	T
I	S	B	E	W	E	I	R	D	P	O

2 Replace the phrases in bold with the words below.

- brilliant   - crazy   - freezing   - huge   - spectacular   - ~~weird~~

1 She was wearing a **very strange** _____weird_____ hat.
2 Their father was a **very clever** _____ engineer.
3 Outside it was **very cold and snowy** _____.
4 They live in a **very big** _____ house.
5 The fireworks at the end of the festival were **very exciting to look at** _____.
6 Some of his ideas are **very stupid** _____.

3 Match 1–8 with a–h.

1 file __b__
2 search _____
3 password _____
4 tweet _____
5 upload _____
6 download _____
7 post _____
8 screenshot _____

a copy or move a document from the Internet to your computer
b information that a computer stores as one unit with one name
c secret letters or numbers that you type into a computer so that you can use it
d put a message or image online so that people can see it
e image of something taken from a computer screen
f look for information on a computer, the Internet, etc.
g put a short comment on Twitter
h copy or move a document from your computer to the Internet

4 Circle the correct options.

1 I *uploaded* / *downloaded* / *tweeted* the photos to the website.
2 I can't remember my *screenshot* / *password* / *file* and I can't access my account!
3 Can you take a *file* / *password* / *screenshot* of the error message, please?
4 I *tweeted* / *searched* / *posted* the Internet for information on the subject.
5 You can *download* / *upload* / *tweet* the app from their website.
6 All my important *screenshots* / *files* / *passwords* are on this computer.

GRAMMAR

1 Circle the correct options.

1 If we **reused** / *reuse* more of our plastic, the oceans would be cleaner.

2 Would she feel better if she *would go* / *went* for a run every morning?

3 If you had a thousand dollars, what *would* / *will* you buy?

4 Olivia *would* / *will* get better grades if she paid attention to her spelling.

5 We wouldn't have all these problems if we *take* / *took* better care of our planet.

6 I think my grandad would get really bored if he *would retire* / *retired* now.

2 Complete the second conditional sentences with the correct form of the verbs in parentheses.

1 She _would make_ (make) more progress if she _took_ (take) a course.

2 I think Rafael _____ (be) healthier if he _____ (do) more exercise.

3 If I _____ (have) more time, I _____ (play) in a band.

4 Most people _____ (be) happier if they _____ (work) less.

5 If we _____ (reduce) the amount of food we bought, we _____ (not waste) so much.

6 Noah _____ (have) more money if he _____ (get) a job.

3 Complete the dialogues with the words below.

• ~~anyone~~   • anything   • anywhere   • someone   • something   • somewhere

A Did you meet your friends at the mall?

B No, I didn't meet ¹_____anyone_____ . I was looking for ²_____ for Ethan's birthday, but I couldn't find ³_____ I liked.

A Maybe the mall is the wrong place for Ethan. Perhaps you should go ⁴_____ else to look for a present.

B Well, at the moment I'm looking for my glasses. They're not in my bedroom, the living room, or the kitchen. I can't find them ⁵_____!

A Maybe ⁶_____ moved them? You often leave them on the floor.

4 Match 1–6 with a–f.

1 She posted __e__   a someone in the yard.

2 I never go _____   b anything to help.

3 I didn't tell _____   c anyone about the problem.

4 He never does _____   d somewhere else.

5 I'm sure I saw _____   e something about the president.

6 It's noisy here. Let's go _____   f anywhere without my phone.

 **READING**

1 Read the text quickly and check (✓) the correct answers.

1 Which sentence is the best description of the article?
- ○ Most young people are rejecting social media.
- ○ Some young people are rejecting social media.
- ○ All young people love using social media.

2 How many young people describe their experiences in the article?
- ○ two   ○ three   ○ four

● ● ●

MEET THE YOUNG PEOPLE WHO REJECT SOCIAL MEDIA

We often hear about young people who live their lives through social media, but some young people are finding that they're happier without it.

Victor, a 16-year-old student from Brasília, rejected social media when he noticed that his classmates were busy texting and reading messages from each other, but not speaking. "People weren't even calling each other. Face-to-face communication just wasn't happening. I thought, this is silly. Social media isn't improving our lives – it's making them worse! I'm going to do things differently."

For 15-year-old Maria Pereira, things changed while she was in a café with some friends. "Three of us were enjoying ourselves, chatting while we ate lunch," she says, "but one of our friends was looking at her phone the whole time. Basically, she was posting online pictures of the food we were eating and then counting the number of likes she got.

We were all talking to each other, but she wasn't paying attention to anything that anyone was saying. She wasn't even eating. It was crazy! I decided then that I would stop using social media."

Other young people are choosing to take a break from social media. 17-year-old Lucas stopped using social media three months ago so he could prepare for his exams: "If I had more time, I'd use social media, but right now, my studies are more important."

But although some young people feel they would be happier if social media didn't exist, this isn't true for people of all ages. Some studies suggest that older people are using social media more, for example, to communicate with family members who live far away. For these people, social media improves the quality of life.

2 Read the text and complete each sentence with one word.

1 Victor noticed that his friends weren't _____speaking_____ to each other.
2 Maria decided to stop using social media one day when she was in a _____.
3 One of Maria's friends was _____ pictures of her food online during lunch.
4 She wasn't paying _____ to the conversation.
5 Lucas stopped using social media so he could study for his _____.
6 Studies show that some _____ people are now using social media more.

3 Write answers to the questions.

1 Why weren't Victor's friends speaking to each other?
_____They were busy texting and reading messages from each other._____

2 What was Maria's friend counting in the café?
----

3 What is more important to Lucas than social media?
----

4 What are some older people using social media for?
----

5 What does social media do to some older people's lives?

6

THE WORLD OF MUSIC

 LANGUAGE REFERENCE

Past Progressive: Affirmative and Negative

Affirmative (+)	Negative (–)
I've lived abroad.	I haven't lived abroad.
I have lived abroad.	I've never lived abroad.
You've written several books.	You haven't written any books.
You have written several books.	You've never written any books.
She's been to a few concerts.	She hasn't been to any concerts.
She has been to a few concerts.	She's never been to any concerts.
We've seen all of her movies.	We haven't seen her movies.
We have seen all of her movies.	We've never seen her movies.
They've heard a lot of jazz.	They haven't heard any jazz.
They have heard a lot of jazz.	They've never heard any jazz.

If we say when the action happened, we use the simple past, not the present perfect.

Present Perfect: Questions and Short Answers

Yes/No Questions (?)	Have you ever been to the US? Has Alan read any of his books? Have they finished school?	Yes, I have. / No, I haven't. Yes, he has. /No, he hasn't. Yes, they have. / No, they haven't.
Wh– Questions (?)	What have you done this week? How has the area changed? How many murals have they painted?	

Types of Music

classical music	pop
country music	R & B (rhythm and blues)
heavy metal	reggae
hip-hop	rock
jazz	techno

Musical Instruments

drums	keyboard
flute	saxophone
French horn	trumpet
guitar	violin

VOCABULARY

1 Circle seven more types of music.

bit classical zopreggaeslkihip-hopairockoiupcountryeiytjazzbipopaoR&Bwutechnopo

1 _____classical_____   3 _____   5 _____   7 _____

2 _____   4 _____   6 _____   8 _____

2 Match 1–6 with a–f.

1 jazz ___c___   3 country music _____   5 hip-hop _____

2 classical music _____   4 heavy metal _____   6 techno _____

3 Label the images with the correct musical instruments.

_____drums_____ | _____ | _____ | _____

_____ | _____ | _____ | _____

4 Match 1–8 with a–h.

1 trumpet ___g___

2 guitar _____

3 keyboard _____

4 drums _____

5 French horn _____

6 violin _____

7 saxophone _____

8 flute _____

a long metal instrument that you blow into while pressing small parts

b instrument with strings that you play with your fingers

c wooden instrument that you hold against your neck and play by moving a stick across strings

d metal instrument with a circular tube that you blow into

e electronic instrument similar to a piano

f round instruments that you hit with your hand or a stick

g metal instrument that you blow into with three buttons

h instrument that you hold to the side of your mouth and blow into

💬 GRAMMAR

1 Check (✓) the correct sentences.

1 a ○ I never went skiing in my life.

   b ○ I've never been skiing in my life.

2 a ○ I've learned to play the guitar when I was a child.

   b ○ I learned to play the guitar when I was a child.

3 a ○ The tree in your yard is so tall now – it really grew!

   b ○ The tree in your yard is so tall now – it's really grown!

4 a ○ He changed his password yesterday.

   b ○ He's changed his password yesterday.

5 a ○ We didn't have dinner at home last night.

   b ○ We haven't had dinner at home last night.

2 What have Juliana, Luis and Marcos done? What have they never done? Write sentences using the prompts.

Juliana / go to / a heavy metal concert ✓

Juliana's been to a heavy metal concert.

Juliana / go to / a classical music concert ✗

Juliana's never been to a classical music concert.

Juliana / play / soccer ✗

_____

_____

Juliana / play / tennis ✓

_____

_____

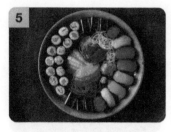   

Luis and Marcos / eat / Japanese food ✗

_____

_____

Luis and Marcos / eat / Italian food ✓

_____

_____

Luis and Marcos / do gymnastics ✓

_____

_____

Luis and Marcos / do yoga ✗

_____

_____

3 Complete the mini dialogues with one word.

A ¹ _____Have_____ you ever baked cookies?

B No, I ² _____.

A ³ _____ Logan and Antonio arrived?

B Yes, they ⁴ _____.

A ⁵ _____ Mia been to the UK?

B No, she ⁶ _____.

4 Complete the dialogue with the correct form of the verbs below.

• be   • ~~do~~   • do   • go   • study   • take

A What have you ¹ _____done_____ today, Amelia?

B Well, I've ² _____ most of the day, actually – mainly geography and history. I ³ _____ a break at lunch – I went to the park and met Mason. What about you? Have you ⁴ _____ busy?

A Yes, I have. I've ⁵ _____ a lot of exercise. I ⁶ _____ for a run this morning and then I did some yoga. I did my math homework, too.

 **READING**

1 Read the text quickly and check (✓) the correct answers.

1 What's unusual about the band that Katy finds out about?
- ○ They practice a lot.
- ○ Their instruments are made from trash.
- ○ They play a lot of different music.

2 What type of music do they play?
- ○ jazz
- ○ rock
- ○ jazz, rock, and reggae

THIS WEEK, ONE OF OUR YEAR 8 STUDENTS, KATY, MET NATALIA AND ETHAN FROM THE BAND RECYCLABEATS TO TALK ABOUT THEIR UNUSUAL MUSIC.

KATY Could you tell us about your band, Natalia?

NATALIA Sure. Basically, we play musical instruments that we've made from things people have thrown away. For example, this violin that I'm holding – Ethan and I made this from an oil can and a few other bits that we found.

KATY That's amazing! You played it for me just now and it sounds really good!

ETHAN Thank you!

KATY And how would you describe the music that you play?

ETHAN Well, generally, we like to play music that people can dance to, but it's a mixture of styles, really – some jazz, some rock, even reggae.

KATY Nice! And where have you played?

ETHAN We've played all over the country, actually. We've performed in towns and schools, at parties, and even at one or two festivals.

KATY Cool! When did you start recycling materials to make instruments?

ETHAN Well, I've made instruments from trash as long as I can remember. My mom was really into recycling – she hates wasting stuff – so when I was little, we made drums from empty cans and parts of balloons. They weren't the best drums I've ever played, but I was very happy with them. One summer, she even made me a guitar from an old box.

KATY Wow, she was very creative!

NATALIA But to be honest, the most important thing in a band is the people, not the instruments. We all love playing together and we make sure we practice a lot, so we make a great sound.

KATY I know you do – I've heard you! Ethan and Natalia, thank you so much for talking to me today!

---

2 Read the text and complete each sentence with one word.

1 The band use instruments made from things that people have ___thrown___ away.

2 They use a _____ which was made from an old oil can.

3 Ethan describes their music as a _____ of different styles.

4 Ethan's _____ made instruments for him when he was a child.

5 She made drums from empty cans and a guitar from an old _____.

6 Natalia says the _____ in a band are more important than the instruments.

3 Write answers to the questions.

1 Where has the band played?
_____They've played in towns and schools, at parties, and at festivals._____

2 What instrument did Natalia play for Katy?
_____

3 What does Ethan's mother not like?
_____

4 How does Katy describe Ethan's mother?
_____

5 Why does Natalia think the band sound so good?
_____

7 AFRICA: PAST, PRESENT, AND FUTURE

 LANGUAGE REFERENCE

Present Perfect with *Already*, *Just*, and *Yet*

Already	Just	Yet
No food for me, thanks. **I've already eaten.** I offered to lend Sara the book, but she**'s already read** it. It's a new disease, but scientists **have already developed** a vaccine.	Jack is definitely here. **I've just seen** him. I'm calling to say we**'ve just arrived.** It was sunny this afternoon, but it **has just started** raining.	They **haven't organized** their vacation **yet.** She **hasn't taken** the exam **yet.** **Have** you **had** lunch **yet?** **Has** Jose **decided** if he's coming **yet?**

Use *already* and *just* after *have/has*.

Present Perfect with *Since* and *For*

Since	For
I've lived in Berlin **since** 2020. We**'ve been** here **since** three o'clock. It**'s snowed since** we arrived. They**'ve had** their cat **since** William was four.	**I've lived** in Italy **for** three years. He**'s studied** there **for** five years. She**'s known** Alexis **for** a long time.

Questions and Answers

How long has he **lived** abroad? He's lived abroad **for** five years. / He's lived abroad **since** he was 10.

How long have you **had** this bike? **For** two years. / **Since** last summer.

Achievements

achieve
achievement
construct
construction
develop
development
discover

discovery
organize
organization
produce
production
survive
survival

Adjectives + Prepositions

afraid of
famous for
good at
interested in
proud of
tired of

 **VOCABULARY**

1 Complete the sentences with the words below. Use the correct form of the verbs.

- ~~achieve/achievement~~   • construct/construction   • discover/discovery   • produce/production

1 a To win a silver medal at the Olympics at the age of 17 was a fantastic __achievement.__

b After seven years of studying, she finally ____achieved____ her ambition to become a doctor.

2 a The _____ of oil during this decade changed the country's economy.

b I recently _____ that my grandma's grandfather was Italian.

3 a The _____ of the mall took two years.

b They decided to _____ a bridge across the river.

4 a In the past, they _____ a lot of cheese in this region.

b We use water in the _____ of almost all products.

2 Put the letters in the correct order and complete the sentences.

1 These plants cannot _____survive_____ (vivruse) in very cold weather.

2 She works for an _____ (roganationiz) that helps immigrants to find homes and work.

3 It sometimes takes years for a company to _____ (vedelpo) a new product.

4 He owns a company that _____ (narogizes) music festivals.

5 They were responsible for the _____ (elopdevment) of a cure.

3 Complete the sentences with the correct words. Then match sentences 1–6 with the correct image (a–f).

1 My older sister is proud __of__ her baking. __e__

2 Isaac is good _____ swimming. _____

3 My cousin is afraid _____ the dark. _____

4 Italy is famous _____ its art. _____

5 Martha's interested _____ photography. _____

6 He's tired _____ doing the same job. _____

a	b	c
d	e	f

4 Rewrite the sentences using the phrases in Exercise 3.

1 The children were pleased with their mural.

_____The children were proud of their mural._____

2 Victoria runs well.

_____

3 My brother gets very anxious when he sees spiders.

_____

4 Switzerland has mountains that everyone knows about.

_____

5 I'm bored because I eat the same sandwiches every day.

_____

6 I always want to hear about the music industry.

_____

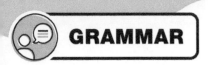

GRAMMAR

1 Circle the correct options.

> Hey, I've ¹*yet* / *just* seen your photo – thanks! Good to hear from you! 11:20 pm

> Hi! Sorry, I've only ²*already* / *just* got back from the US. 😎 We had an amazing time. 11:20 pm

> Great! I want to hear all about it next Friday! Today's going to be busy. Pedro and I are throwing a surprise birthday party for a friend this evening, but we haven't organized everything ³*yet* / *already*. 11:21 pm

> Oh no! 😨 11:21 pm

> Well, we've ⁴*yet* / *already* bought everything, but we haven't cooked anything ⁵*just* / *yet*. 11:21 pm

> What about the 🎁 ? 11:22 pm

> Oh yes, Pedro's ⁶*already* / *yet* bought the present! 11:22 pm

2 Write sentences using the prompts and the correct form of the present perfect.

1 he / already / achieve / his ambition .

_____He's already achieved his ambition_____

2 I / just / upload / the file .

_____

3 she / not / leave home / yet .

_____

4 they / already / destroy / half of the rainforest .

_____

5 you / finish school / yet ?

_____

6 she / post / any photos online ?

_____

3 Complete the sentences with *for* or *since*.

1 I haven't drunk anything __since__ breakfast!

2 They haven't flown _____ three years.

3 She's played soccer _____ she was six.

4 I've had these shoes _____ four years.

5 We've recycled plastic here _____ over two decades.

6 They have studied science _____ they were ten.

4 Write questions and answers using the prompts and *for* or *since*.

1 Q have a skateboard? _____How long has he had a skateboard?_____

A a year _____For a year_____

2 Q work in a café? _____

A February _____

3 Q be married? _____

A last summer _____

4 Q study math? _____

A 13 years _____

 **READING**

1 Read the text quickly and check (✓) the correct answers.

1 What's the article about?
- ○ Silicon Valley, California
- ○ new technology in Africa
- ○ the problem of old technology

2 What's a technology hub?
- ○ building or buildings where technology companies work together
- ○ city with a lot of technology companies
- ○ country with a lot of technology companies

Africa's tech hub success

If someone asked you where the newest technology came from, what would you reply? If you answered "Silicon Valley, California" you'd be right, of course, but did you know that Africa is also helping to develop some of the next generation of technology?

A lot of this new technology is the result of technology hubs which are starting up all over Africa. A technology hub (or tech hub) is a place that has developed to help small technology companies achieve their goals. It can be one building or a group of buildings, but the idea is that people from different tech companies come together to share their ideas as well as their equipment. Many of these tech hubs are in the countries of Nigeria, South Africa, and Egypt, but they are present in a lot of other countries across the continent. They

are mainly in the bigger cities but also in some of the smaller ones.

So why have these tech hubs started up in recent years? One reason is that Africa has a very young population. Over 75% of its people are under 35. Young people are often interested in innovative technology and they're not afraid of it. They're also generally very good at it.

Another reason is that parts of Africa already benefit from recent technology. Other areas of the world are still using systems that they developed ten or fifteen years ago. In parts of Africa, they didn't have the previous generation of technology and they're now using the newest and most advanced systems.

In future, the technology in our phones and our computers may well come from a technology hub in Africa.

2 Read the text and write *T* (true) or *F* (false) next to the statements.

1 New technology doesn't come from California. ___F___
2 Some new technology comes from Africa. _____
3 A lot of technology hubs are in three countries in Africa. _____
4 The hubs are only in the big cities in Africa. _____
5 Africa has very many young people. _____
6 Parts of Africa have more advanced technology than other areas of the world. _____

3 Write answers to the questions.

1 What two things can companies share in a technology hub?
_____They can share ideas and equipment._____

2 Which three African countries are many of these tech hubs in?
_____

3 How many people in Africa are under 35?
_____

4 What does the writer say young people are often interested in?
_____

5 What are other parts of the world still using?
_____

8 WHAT'S IMPORTANT TO ME?

 LANGUAGE REFERENCE

Present Perfect vs. Simple Past

Unspecified Time in the Past	My grandad **has achieved** a lot in his life. Ice cream is my favorite food. I**'ve** always **loved** it. They**'ve lived** there for a long time. We**'ve visited** them **several times**.
Specific Time in the Past	I **worked** hard **yesterday** and **achieved** a lot. I **loved** ice cream **when I was little**. They **lived** there **from 2015 to 2021**. We **visited** them **last year**.

If there is a word/phrase saying when the action happened, for example *yesterday*, *last year*, *two days ago*, we don't use the present perfect.

Subject and Object Questions

Subject Questions	Object Questions
What **wakes** her so early in the morning?	Why **does** she **get up** so early?
Who **bakes** the cookies?	What **does** he **bake**?
How many people **came** to the party?	How many people **did** you **invite**?
What **happened** to the trees?	When **did** they **cut down** the trees?
Who **called** Nicole just now?	Who **did** Nicole **call** just now?

Phrases with *Do*, *Have*, and *Make*

do your best
do physical activities
do the shopping
do volunteer work
do well
have an opportunity

have time
have trouble
make decisions
make a difference
make mistakes
make money

Verbs + Prepositions

belong to
care about
deal with
fight for
suffer from
work for

VOCABULARY

1 Complete the sentences with the correct form of *do, have,* and *make*. Then match images a–f with sentences 1–6.

1 The students _____had_____ an opportunity to _____ some volunteer work last spring. ___b___

2 She was _____ some trouble with a few girls at school. _____

3 He _____ some mistakes. He didn't read the instructions properly. _____

4 Try to find time to _____ some physical activities. _____

5 They always _____ a lot of money when the weather is hot. _____

6 Amanda _____ the shopping last weekend. _____

2 Complete the text with the correct form of *do, have,* and *make.*

The last two years have been so busy with exams – I really haven't ¹_____had_____ time for anything else. For example, last year I ²_____ an opportunity to do some voluntary work at a bird sanctuary and I'm really interested in birds, but I finally decided not to do it. I always find it hard to ³_____ decisions but it was the correct one. I was able to study hard and ⁴_____ my best – I ⁵_____ really well in my exams. And the future? I don't want to ⁶_____ a lot of money. I want to ⁷_____ a difference – probably working to protect the environment. That's the plan!

3 Circle the correct options.

1 Ella belongs *with /* (*to*) a running club.

2 The environment is our future. We should all care *with / about* it!

3 She fought *for / about* women's right to vote.

4 He suffered *for / from* a very rare disease.

5 We've had to deal *about / with* so many problems recently.

6 James works *to / for* a company that makes office furniture.

4 Match 1–6 with a–f.

1 She fights ___d___   a for the same company.

2 I don't have time to deal _____   b about me and want me to be happy.

3 Sam and Luke both work _____   c with the contract today.

4 He was suffering _____   d for girls' right to education.

5 My sister belongs _____   e from cancer at the time.

6 I know my parents care _____   f to a book club.

GRAMMAR

1 Circle the correct options.

1 You swim very well now! You *have really improved* / *really improved*!

2 Their children *left home* / *have left home* many years ago.

3 She *finished* / *has finished* school last July.

4 I *lost* / *have lost* my headphones. Please could you help me look for them?

5 He *arrived* / *has arrived* in Mexico in 2020.

6 Julia *has known* / *knew* George since they were five years old.

2 Complete the dialogue with the correct present perfect or simple past form of the verbs in parentheses.

José   When ¹ *did you come* (you come) to London, Paolo?

Paolo   I ² _____ (arrive) here two years ago, but before that, I ³ _____ (live) in Germany from 2017 to 2020.

José   So you ⁴ _____ (be) in Europe for several years?

Paolo   Yes, that's right. What about you?

José   I ⁵ _____ (live) here for a year. I ⁶ _____ (start) a job at the university last June.

3 Read the sentences and write S (subject questions) or O (object questions).

1 Who told you it was my birthday? _S_

2 What did Thomas Edison invent? _____

3 How many museums did you visit? _____

4 What did Gemma say? _____

5 What happened to this vase? _____

6 How did you get to the beach? _____

7 Who took this photo? _____

8 What persuades people to buy things? _____

4 Write a subject question (SQ) and an object question (OQ) for each sentence.

1 Carmen painted an amazing picture.

SQ: _____ Who painted an amazing picture? _____

OQ: _____ What did Carmen paint? _____

2 Rebecca made Manuel's birthday cake.

SQ: _____

OQ: _____

3 The festival started three days ago.

SQ: _____

OQ: _____

4 Sylva won the gold medal.

SQ: _____

OQ: _____

 **READING**

1 Read the text quickly and check (✓) the correct answers.

1 What's the interview about?
- ○ two teenagers' relationships with their parents
- ○ the most important people in the lives of two teenagers
- ○ why friends are more important than family

2 What do Arthur and Isabella mention?
- ○ family
- ○ friends
- ○ friends and family

As part of our "focus on teens" feature, Wilson Field spoke to Arthur (15) and Isabella (14) about the people in their lives that are most important to them. Their answers were interesting. Below is part of the interview.

Wilson So, Arthur and Isabella, tell me about the most important people in your lives. Who do you value the most?

Arthur My mom, definitely. She's amazing. She works really hard, but she's always had time for me. When I had some trouble at school and I needed someone to talk to, she was there for me, even when she was very busy. She's really cool.

Isabella And for me, friends are super-important. I can talk to them about things that I can't discuss with my mom or dad. And I really enjoy hanging out with them. Of course, my parents are important, too. Whatever mistakes I make, they still love me. That's not true for many people in your life, even your best friends!

Wilson Very true! And who has influenced you most? Arthur, I understand you're an artist – a very good painter. So, who noticed that you could paint and encouraged you to do it? Was it a parent or a teacher?

Arthur No, it wasn't, actually. It was my best friend's dad – he paints fantastic murals. I was drawing a picture at my friend's house when I was seven or eight and he said something nice about it. I knew he was an artist so it really gave me confidence. And he's been interested in my art ever since then. Just last week, I showed him one of my paintings and he gave me some really good advice. So he's definitely made a difference to my life. Yes, he's been important to me, too.

2 Read the text and check (✓) who says these things.

		Arthur	Isabella
1	Their mother is the most important person in their life.	✓	
2	They had problems when they were younger and needed to talk about them.		
3	They can't talk about some subjects with their mother and father.		
4	They enjoy spending time with their friends.		
5	If they do something bad or silly, their parents won't stop loving them.		
6	A friend's parent has been important in their life.		

3 Write answers to the questions.

1 What two adjectives does Arthur use to describe his mom?

  He says she's amazing and cool.

2 Which person doesn't mention their father?

  ----

3 Who are the most important people for Isabella?

  ----

4 How old was Arthur when someone noticed that he was good at drawing?

  ----

5 Who has had a very strong influence on Arthur's art?

Thanks and Acknowledgements

We would like to thank the following people for their invaluable contribution to the series:

Ruth Atkinson, Lauren Fenton, Tom Hadland, Meredith Levy, Cara Norris, Lynne Robertson, Maria Toth, Kate Woodford and Liz Walter.

The authors and editors would like to thank all the teachers who have contributed to the development of the course:

Geysla Lopes de Alencar, Priscila Araújo, David Williams Mocock de Araújo, Leticia da Silva Azevedo, Francisco Evangelista Ferreira Batista, Luiz Fernando Carmo, Thiago Silva Campos, Cintia Castilho, Mônica Egydio, Érica Fernandes, Viviane Azevêdo de Freitas, Marco Giovanni, Rodolfo de Aro da Rocha Keizer, Vanessa Leroy, Bruno Fernandes de Lima, Allana Tavares Maciel, Jonadab Mansur, Rogério dos Santos Melo, Carlos Ubiratã Gois de Menezes, Aryanne Moreira, Joelba Geane da Silva, Vanessa Silva Pereira, Daniela Costa Pinheiro, Isa de França Vasconcelos, Eliana Perrucci Vergani, Geraldo Vieira, Whebston Mozart.

The authors and publishers acknowledge the following sources of copyright material and are grateful for the permissions granted. While every effort has been made, it has not always been possible to identify the sources of all the material used, or to trace all copyright holders. If any omissions are brought to our notice, we will be happy to include the appropriate acknowledgements on reprinting and in the next update to the digital edition, as applicable.

Key: R = Review, U = Unit, WU = Welcome unit.

Student's Book

Photography

All the photos are sourced from Getty Images.

WU: Andrea Pistolesi/Stone; Hello Lovely/Corbis; Sarah Casillas/DigitalVision; SolStock/E+; LanaStock/iStock/Getty Images Plus; David Engelhardt; Carlos Ciudad Photography/Moment; Byronsdad/E+; WLADIMIR BULGAR/SCIENCE PHOTO LIBRARY/Science Photo Library; Beau Van Der Graaf/EyeEm; Warren Faidley/The Image Bank; Peter Cade/Stone; Kritchanut/iStock/Getty Images Plus; Sollina Images/The Image Bank; Shumoff/iStock Editorial/Getty Images Plus; JohnnyGreig/E+; Chan Srithaweeporn/Moment; PeopleImages/E+; **U1:** martin-dm/E+; skynesher/E+; IPGGutenbergUKLtd/iStock/Getty Images Plus; Terry Vine/The Image Bank; SDI Productions/E+; Prostock-Studio/iStock/Getty Images Plus; JohnnyGreig/E+; kali9/e+; Andreas Debus/EyeEm; Mike Kemp; Image Source; Juanmonino/iStock/Getty Images Plus; Igor Alecsander/E+; WLADIMIR BULGAR/Science Photo Library/Getty Images Plus; AaronAmat/iStock/Getty Images Plus; masterSergeant/Stock/Getty Images Plus; damircudic/E+; nlStock/E+; Neustockimages/E+; Jessie sson/DigitalVision; MARTY MELVILLE/ ; MachineHeadz/iStock/Getty Images **U2:** monkeybusinessimages/iStock/Images Plus; Nick David/Stone; vgajic/ phen Swintek/Stone; DejanKolar/E+; t Studios/DigitalVision; M_a_y_a/ ot; svetikd/E+; Thomas Barwick/ n; MamiGibbs/Moment; wweagle/ Kingham/Cultura; Sabine Mederer/tographed by Marko Natri/Moment; /Stone; Lilli Day/Photodisc; fStop

Images - Larry Washburn/Brand X Pictures; Yagi Studio/DigitalVision; alashi/DigitalVision Vectors; Ponomariova_Maria/iStock/Getty Images Plus; JGI/Jamie Grill; Juanmonino/E+; DAJ; Danny Lehman/The Image Bank; Marija Jovovic/E+; FatCamera/E+; Vostok/Moment; SDI Productions/E+; oxygen/Moment; Juj Winn/Moment; Charles O'Rear/Corbis Documentary; Yaroslav Kushta/Moment; BremecR/E+; Severinas Ziukas/EyeEm; kbeis/DigitalVision Vectors; yuoak/DigitalVision Vectors; Tanya St/iStock/Getty Images Plus; **R1&2:** SDI Productions/E+; Barry Winiker/The Image Bank Unreleased; Denkou Images/Cultura; Ridofranz/iStock/Getty Images Plus; ChristopherBernard/E+; RapidEye/E+; filo/DigitalVision Vectors; **U3:** dorian2013/iStock/Getty Images Plus; nikom1234/iStock/Getty Images Plus; Peter Dazeley/The Image Bank; Brilly/DigitalVision Vectors; Jamie Grill; pixelfit/E+; milindri/iStock/Getty Images Plus; author/iStock/Getty Images Plus; Tasha Vector/iStock/Getty Images Plus; Peter Cade/Stone; Federico Candoni/EyeEm; Ben Gingell/iStock/Getty Images Plus; DrAfter123/DigitalVision Vectors; Malte Mueller; exxorian/DigitalVision Vectors; smartboy10/DigitalVision Vectors; Carl Court/Staff/Getty Images News; Lena Clara; Westend61; SDI Productions/E+; Roos Koole/Moment; **U4:** peepo/E+; ET-ARTWORKS/DigitalVision Vectors; pixelfusion3d/DigitalVision Vectors; filo/DigitalVision Vectors; OnnoIllustration/DigitalVision Vectors; leila_divine/iStock/Getty Images Plus; South_agency/DigitalVision Vectors; VectorPocket/iStock/Getty Images Plus; Alina Kvaratskhelia/iStock/Getty Images Plus; naqiewei/DigitalVision Vectors; drmakkoy/DigitalVision Vectors; apomares/E+; Oxford Scientific/Photodisc; bob van den berg photography/Moment Open; Heritage Images/Hulton Archive; antonios mitsopoulos/Moment; cjmckendry/E+; Marco Bottigelli/Moment; sandsun/iStock/Getty Images Plus; girlfrommars/iStock/Getty Images Plus; sabelskaya/iStock/Getty Images Plus; **R3&4:** Oscar Wong/Moment; Ratsanai/DigitalVision Vectors; hudiemm/DigitalVision Vectors; designer29/DigitalVision Vectors; BRIAN MITCHELL/Corbis Documentary; Elvinagraph/iStock/Getty Images Plus; FrankRamspott/DigitalVision Vectors; **U5:** metamorworks/iStock/Getty Images Plus; jamielawton/DigitalVision Vectors; Pablo Benedito/Aurora Photos; Hendry Wijayanto/iStock/Getty Images Plus; ET-ARTWORKS/DigitalVision Vectors; Colin Anderson Productions pty ltd/DigitalVision; Eva Almqvist/iStock/Getty Images Plus; David Wall/Moment; moisseyev/iStock/Getty Images Plus; vitalik19111992/iStock/Getty Images Plus; Stocktrek Images; TED ALJIBE/AFP; Houda Chaloun/EyeEm; worklater1/iStock/Getty Images Plus; andreusK/iStock/Getty Images Plus; ViewStock; sturti/iStock/Getty Images Plus; appleuzr/DigitalVision Vectors; rambo182/DigitalVision Vectors; cnythzl/DigitalVision Vectors; Esra Sen Kula/DigitalVision Vectors; lumpynoodles/DigitalVision Vectors; Amin Yusifov/iStock/Getty Images Plus; SDI Productions/E+; alengo/E+; wagnerokasaki/E+; Christian Petersen-Clausen/Moment Unreleased; VICTOR HABBICK VISIONS/SCIENCE PHOTO LIBRARY; VioletaStoimenova/E+; **U6:** ivosevicv/E+; mecaleha/DigitalVision Vectors; skynesher/E+; Joey Foley/Getty Images Entertainment; Henrik Sorensen/DigitalVision; Westend61; Niklas Skur/EyeEm; Comstock/Stockbyte; Chris Polk/AMA2017/Getty Images Entertainment; Leontura/DigitalVision Vectors; undefined/iStock/Getty Images Plus; scanrail/

iStock/Getty Images Plus; Llgorko/iStock/Getty Images Plus; Ugo Ambroggio/EyeEm; pixhook/E+; -M-I-S-H-A-/iStock/Getty Images Plus; ERphotographer/iStock/Getty Images Plus; sihuo0860371/iStock/Getty Images Plus; Imgorthand/E+; Sumit Pandit/EyeEm; Chuck Savage/The Image Bank Unreleased; vm/E+; kali9/E+; monkeybusinessimages/iStock/Getty Images Plus; CribbVisuals/iStock Unreleased; Jemal Countess/WireImage; Barry King/Sygma; Time Life Pictures/The LIFE Picture Collection; Rico D'Rozario/Redferns; Silver Screen Collection/Moviepix; **R5&6:** Perkus/E+; Bombaert Patrick/EyeEm; MortenBjerregaard/Getty Images Plus; Sergiy1975/iStock/Getty Images Plus; RapidEye/E+; Elisa Bistocchi/EyeEm; Tetra Images; RodrigoBlanco/E+; Roy JAMES Shakespeare/Photodisc; **U7:** Tim White/The Image Bank; Buena Vista Images/Photodisc; Avatar_023/iStock/Getty Images Plus; kimberrywood/DigitalVision Vectors; Richard Clark/The Image Bank; David Malan; bubaone/DigitalVision Vectors; Keith Lance/iStock/Getty Images Plus; Eric Lafforgue/Art in All of Us/Corbis News; JOUAN/RIUS/Gamma-Rapho; Eric LAFFORGUE Suresh/Gamma-Rapho; Krishna/Moment; Westend61; Geraint Rowland Photography/Moment; Yadira G. Morel/Moment; DEA/C. DANI & I. JESKE/De Agostini; Hoberman Collection/Universal Images Group; SDI Productions/E+; **U8:** Johner Images; olaser/E+; JulNichols/E+; smartboy10/DigitalVision Vectors; sorbetto/DigitalVision Vectors; fjmoura/DigitalVision Vectors; VasjaKoman/DigitalVision Vectors; Feodora Chiosea/iStock/Getty Images Plus; Nick David/Photodisc; South_agency/E+; Thinkstock Images/Stockbyte; Jasmin Merdan/Moment; fstop123/iStock/Getty Images Plus; recep-bg/E+; Pawel Libera/LightRocket; DianaHirsch/E+; Roberto Lo Savio/EyeEm; johnwoodcock/DigitalVision Vectors; Radoslav Zilinsky/Moment; Robert Kneschke/EyeEm; Frans Lemmens/Corbis Documentary; Mikael Vaisanen/The Image Bank; Westend61; **R7&8:** kali9/iStock/Getty Images Plus; Aleksandar Jankovic/iStock/Getty Images Plus; martinedoucet/E+; **END:** Yagi Studio/Stone; rez-art/iStock/Getty Images Plus; Pgiam/E+; Joel Papalini/EyeEm; AzmanJaka/E+; eZeePics Studio/iStock Editorial; Education Images/Universal Images Group; MrPlumo/DigitalVision Vectors; Skathi/iStock/Getty Images Plus; bubaone/DigitalVision Vectors; Bolsunova/iStock/Getty Images Plus; PIUS UTOMI EKPEI/AFP; Universal Images Group; Indianapolis Museum of Art at Newfields/Archive Photos; Vadym Plysiuk/iStock/Getty Images Plus; Hill Street Studios/DigitalVision; SDI Productions/E+; Jasmin Merdan/Moment; Ariel Skelley/DigitalVision; Morsa Images/E+; miakievy/DigitalVision Vectors.

Workbook

Photography

U1: PeopleImages/E+; Terry Vine/DigitalVision; Hans Neleman/Stone; Klaus Vedfelt/DigitalVision; Fotografo/iStock/Getty Images Plus; Simon Winnall/The Image Bank; Nancy Honey/Cultura; Tim Hall/Cultura; Letizia Le Fur/ONOKY; DragonImages/iStock/Getty Images Plus; Alistair Berg/DigitalVision; sturti/E+; lupengyu/Moment; gorica/iStock/Getty Images Plus; davidcreacion/iStock/Getty Images Plus; **U2:** martin-dm/E+; barsik/iStock/Getty Images Plus; Alex Liew/E+; Westend61; SolStock/E+; skynesher/iStock/Getty Images Plus; **U3:** gorica/iStock/Getty Images Plus; yayayoyo/iStock/

143